essential assessment

Mathematics

National Curriculum practice tests
End Key Stage 2

Text © Sean McArdle 1996, 2001

The right of Sean McArdle to be identified as author of this work has been asserted by him in accordance with the Copyright, Designs and Patents Act 1988.

All rights reserved. The copyright holders authorise ONLY users of *Essential Assessment: Maths Keystage 2, Book 1* to make photocopies or stencil duplicates of the photocopiable worksheets on pages 12-128 for their own or their classes' immediate use within the teaching context. No other rights are granted without permission in writing from the publishers or under licence from the Copyright Licensing Agency Limited. Further details of such licences (for reprographic reproduction) may be obtained from the Copyright Licensing Agency Limited of 90 Tottenham Court Road, London W1P 9HE. Copy by any other means or for any other purpose is strictly prohibited without prior written consent from the copyright holders. Application for such permission should be addressed to the publishers.

First published in 1996 by
Stanley Thornes (Publishers) Ltd

This edition published in 2001 by
Nelson Thornes
Delta Place
27 Bath Road
CHELTENHAM GL53 7TH
United Kingdom

01 02 03 04 05 / 10 9 8 7 6 5 4 3 2 1

A catalogue record for this book is available from the British Library.
ISBN 0-7487-6152-7

Designed by Ian Foulis & Associates, Plymouth, Devon

Printed and bound in Great Britain
by Ashford Colour Press, Gosport, Hampshire.

Contents

Notes on how to set, mark and interpret the tests	4
Answers	7
Test 1	12
Test 2	26
Test 3	40

Practice sheets

Number and algebra level 3	54
Number and algebra level 4	66
Number and algebra level 5	77
Shape, space and measures level 3	89
Shape, space and measures level 4	97
Shape, space and measures level 5	105
Handling data level 3	113
Handling data level 4	121
Handling data level 5	126

Notes on how to set, mark and interpret the tests

These notes are to help the teacher use this book to the best advantage. They aim to explain the ideas behind the book, the contents of the book and the way it may be used. Ultimately it will be the responsibility of each school or teacher to decide how to make use of the following assessments, but a few minutes spent browsing through these notes will help to gain the best advantage from these materials.

The layout of the book
This book is in two sections. The first section is made up of three Key Stage 2 assessment type tests. The second section contains practice pages of questions, graduated according to attainment targets and level descriptions, and again similar in kind to those found in the Key Stage 2 Assessments.

Using the book
The two sections may be used in different ways but the most obvious will be:

1 Set the tests themselves and then base revision upon the results.

2 Make use of the practice exercises first and then set the tests.

3 A combination of the first two points; first some revision using the practice pages, then the first test, then more revision based upon the results of the first test, then the second test, and revision again where necessary.

It should be said that, as with the real Key Stage 2 assessments, each test does not cover the entire Key Stage 2 curriculum, so when a child does well in a test this does not necessarily indicate that they have complete knowledge of the curriculum. However, almost the entire Key Stage 2 mathematics curriculum is covered over the three tests.

The Key Stage 2 practice tests
The tests are not intended to be absolute look-alikes for the real thing as we have included as wide a range of questions as possible. However, they do contain the same sorts of questions as those used at the end of Key Stage 2 and are presented on the page in a similar way so as to familiarise the children with the style of question, the use or non-use of the calculator symbol and the column for recording marks or making comments.

The tests also follow the general pattern of moving from Level 3, through Level 4 towards Level 5, although it may be that parts of the same question cover different levels and attainment targets. Such intermixing of levels and ATs can make marking and trying to find the 'level' of a child very difficult, but nevertheless does represent good practice in teaching mathematics.

Setting the practice tests
Each test is long – 14 pages – and very full, so it is not intended that children should sit the whole assessment in one session. Instead, as mentioned previously, the tests graduate from level to level in three stages so it is best if they are set in that way, probably over a three day period. In this way the children will be able to give of their best without becoming tired and the teacher may have a chance to mark them in smaller sections over a longer period.

The approach suggested above also has the advantage that less able children may be 'entered' for Levels 3 and 4 but not necessarily for the whole test. Thus, when deciding which children in the lower ability stages should be set the tests or the tasks for the official assessments, teachers will be able to base their judgements on some prior testing of a similar kind. Such evidence may also be offered to parents.

Unlike the real assessments, there are no set times in which these tests or parts of tests should be answered. However, given that the tests are likely to be done in three stages, as suggested above, we would recommend that a time of one hour should be allowed for each section. Thus, a total time of three hours needs to be allowed for.

We recommend that the children should sit as far apart as is practicable, preferably at their own desk, that they should do the test in silence and that no teacher intervention should take place during the test. The children will need to have basic equipment of :
　　pencil, ruler, calculator, tracing paper, protractor, rubber
It is also advisable to have a reading book available for those who finish with time to spare.

As with the official assessments, the calculator sign with a tick means it **must** be used, and with a cross means it **must not** be used. If there is no sign, a calculator **may** be used.

The official assessments need all calculations to be shown, other than those where a calculator is allowed. Similarly, the following tests also expect the children to show all working, and the answers are to be written on the page.

Marking the practice tests
A simple marking scheme goes with each test and this gives a clear visual indication of how well each child is progressing and the level which they are attaining. The marked test papers may be used for remediation through the practice pages.

Interpreting the results
The marking sheet for each test gives a very clear indication of how well a child is progressing throughout the Key Stage 2 mathematics curriculum. It tells the teacher exactly where a child has succeeded or failed on a particular test and thus enables remedial work to take place. The combination of the marking sheets for the three tests will clearly show the level of the child although a number of points need to be considered.

1 Unlike the official assessments, the main point of this test is not to end up with one level description grade for each child but rather to allow the children to practise assessments and to give the teacher a chance to help them revise work they are weak on. It is therefore far more important to have an accurate knowledge of where children are failing and a general feeling of how they fit against the level descriptions than simply to know which level number they are.

2 The child does not need to have every part of the questions at any level correct in order to achieve that level or the next one. In other words, a child may get many, though not all, of the questions correct at Level 3 and still be awarded a Level 4 or 5 if successful enough at those levels.

3 The national average for children leaving Key Stage 2 is somewhere within Level 4.

The practice pages
The practice pages are highly focused in order to give extra tests on specific points within the Key Stage 2 mathematics

curriculum. The pages themselves are based upon the 'Dearing' statements and each page can be seen as a test within its own right, or as a section of the curriculum.

The practice pages are categorised by attainment target and by the level, so the teacher can offer very specific assistance to children in the areas where they may be weak. Each page represents a test and may be used with individual children or the whole class at once. We recommend spending between ten and fifteen minutes on each page.

The answers will enable the teacher to pick up very quickly on how well a child is doing and offer assistance before the official test.

Essential Assessments Marking Scheme

The National Curriculum tests in mathematics result in the school and parents being given a simple, one figure number for each child. This number represents the Level which the child has achieved across the whole of mathematics. Key Stage 2 Mathematics Assessments can go up to Level 5 and in some circumstances Level 6, although the average child is awarded a Level 4.

The Level does not relate to any particular aspect of mathematics or even the main Attainment Targets of Number and Algebra, Shape, Space and Measures or Handling Data; it is simply a total score across Levels 3, 4 and 5. Most teachers and parents would see such a figure as being interesting but not very useful. The tests in this book have been designed to be of great use to parents and teachers and to offer a tremendous amount of information which can be acted upon to help each child with any problems which may be shown up by the answers they give in the tests or practice exercises. We emphasise that the single Level number is of little use in taking a child forward.

However, it is recognised that teachers and parents would welcome some indication about which Level a child is at. The following marking scheme is designed to help teachers and parents to find a Level, by giving more detailed information as well as an overall level.

Instructions

1 Mark the test pages and put the score in the relevant circle on the answer sheets as you mark to indicate what has been achieved. The number printed beneath the circle is the total number of marks which can be allocated to that question.

2 Total the number of marks for each category, i.e. Number 3 or Shape 5.

3 Look at the chart below and match the test results with the child's answers; this will give an indication of the child's level.

This chart shows the possible number of marks for each test and may be used for a basic comparison with the child's scores in order to judge success.

TEST 1			TEST 2			TEST 3		
N3 24	S3 19	H3 5	N3 26	S3 15	H3 5	N3 26	S3 5	H3 14
N4 26	S4 8	H4 19	N4 37	S4 9	H4 6	N4 30	S4 11	H4 9
N5 22	S5 15	H5 16	N5 27	S5 13	H5 12	N5 26	S5 20	H5 9

Level 3 marking for Test 1
In order to find out how well the child has achieved across Number and Algebra, Shape, Space and Measure and Handling Data at Level 3, add up the three scores in the boxes N3, S3 and H3.

35 upwards indicates a child working well at Level 3
21–33 indicates a child working within Level 2 and towards Level 3
10–20 indicates some work towards Level 3 with many areas to be addressed
Less than 10 would indicate a child working at Level 2 or below

Level 4 marking for Test 1
In order to find out how well the child has achieved across Number and Algebra, Shape, Space and Measure and Handling Data at Level 4, add up the three scores in the boxes N4, S4 and H4.

44 upwards indicates a child working well at Level 4
28–43 indicates a child working within Level 3 and towards Level 4
16–27 indicates some work towards Level 4 with many areas to be addressed
Less than 16 would indicate a child working at Level 3 or below

Level 5 marking for Test 1
In order to find out how well the child has achieved across Number and Algebra, Shape, Space and Measure and Handling Data at Level 5, add up the three scores in the boxes N5, S5 and H5.

34 upwards indicates a child working within Level5
21–33 indicates a child working within Level 4 and towards Level 5
10–20 indicates some work towards Level 4 with many areas to be addressed
Less than 10 would indicate a child working at Level 3 or below

Marking across Levels in Number and Algebra in Test 1
In order to find out how well the child has achieved within Number and Algebra at Levels 3, 4 and 5 add up the three scores in the boxes N3, N4 and N5.

60 upwards indicates a child working well at Level 5
40–59 indicates a child working within Level 4
19–39 indicates a poor Level 4 or Level 3 with many areas to be addressed
Less than 19 would indicate a child working at Level 3 or below

Marking across Levels in Shape, Space and Measure in Test 1
In order to find out how well the child has achieved within Shape, Space and Measure at Levels 3, 4 and 5 add up the three scores in the boxes S3, S4 and S5.

35 upwards indicates a child working well at Level 5
24–34 indicates a child working within Level 4
14–23 indicates a poor Level 4 or Level 3 with many areas to be addressed
Less than 14 would indicate a child working at Level 3 or below

Marking across Levels in Handling Data in Test 1
In order to find out how well the child has achieved within Handling Data at Levels 3, 4 and 5 add up the three scores in the boxes H3, H4 and H5.

33 upwards indicates a child working well at Level 5
20–32 indicates a child working within Level 4
10–19 indicates a poor Level 4 or Level 3 with many areas to be addressed
Less than 10 would indicate a child working at Level 3 or below

Overall Level for Test 1
If you wish an overall Level score, total the child's scores throughout the test by adding all nine boxes.

123 upwards is a probable Level 5
79–119 is a probable Level 4
39–78 is a probable Level 3
Below 39 means the child could be anywhere within Levels 1 and 2, depending upon their score.

Level 3 marking for Test 2
In order to find out how well the child has achieved across Number and Algebra, Shape, Space and Measure and Handling Data at Level 3, add up the three scores in the boxes N3, S3 and H3.

38 upwards indicates a child working well at Level 3
22–37 indicates a child working within Level 2 and towards Level 3
10–21 indicates some work towards Level 3 with many areas to be addressed
Less than 10 would indicate a child working at Level 2 or below

Level 4 marking for Test 2
In order to find out how well the child has achieved across Number and Algebra, Shape, Space and Measure and Handling Data at Level 4, add up the three scores in the boxes N4, S4 and H4.

44 upwards indicates a child working well at Level 4
28–43 indicates a child working within Level 3 and towards Level 4
16–27 indicates some work towards Level 4 with many areas to be addressed
Less than 16 would indicate a child working at Level 3 or below

Level 5 marking for Test 2
In order to find out how well the child has achieved across Number and Algebra, Shape, Space and Measure and Handling Data at Level 5, add up the three scores in the boxes N5, S5 and H5.

35 upwards indicates a child working well at Level 5
21–34 indicates a child working within Level 4 and towards Level 5
10–20 indicates some work towards Level 5 with many areas to be addressed
Less than 10 would indicate a child working at Level 4 or below

Marking across Levels in Number and Algebra in Test 2
In order to find out how well the child has achieved within Number and Algebra at Levels 3, 4 and 5 add up the three scores in the boxes N3, N4 and N5.

76 upwards indicates a child working well at Level 5
48–75 indicates a child working within Level 4
25–47 indicates a poor Level 4 or Level 3 with many areas to be addressed
Less than 25 would indicate a child working at Level 3 or below

Marking across Levels in Shape, Space and Measure in Test 2
In order to find out how well the child has achieved within Shape, Space and Measure at Levels 3, 4 and 5 add up the three scores in the boxes S3, S4 and S5.

32 upwards indicates a child working well at Level 5
20–31 indicates a child working within Level 4
10–19 indicates a poor Level 4 or Level 3 with many areas to be addressed
Less than 10 would indicate a child working at Level 3 or below

Marking across Levels in Handling Data in Test 2
In order to find out how well the child has achieved within Handling Data at Levels 3, 4 and 5 add up the three scores in the boxes H3, H4 and H5.

18 upwards indicates a child working well at Level 5
10–17 indicates a child working within Level 4
5–9 indicates a poor Level 4 or Level 3 with many areas to be addressed
Less than 5 would indicate a child working at Level 3 or below

Overall Level for Test 2
If you wish an overall Level score, total the child's score throughout the test by adding all nine boxes.

120 upwards is a probable Level 5
79–119 is a probable Level 4
39–78 is a probable Level 3
Below 39 means the child could be anywhere within the band Levels 1 and 2, depending upon their score.

Level 3 marking for Test 3
In order to find out how well the child has achieved across Number and Algebra, Shape, Space and Measure and Handling Data at Level 3, add up the three scores in the boxes N3, S3 and H3.

38 upwards indicates a child working well at Level 3
21–37 indicates a child working within Level 2 and towards Level 3
10–20 indicates some work towards Level 3 with many areas to be addressed
Less than 10 would indicate a child working at Level 2 or below

Level 4 marking for Test 3
In order to find out how well the child has achieved across Number and Algebra, Shape, Space and Measure and Handling Data at Level 4, add up the three scores in the boxes N4, S4 and H4.

42 upwards indicates a child working well at Level 4
28–41 indicates a child working within Level 3 and towards Level 4
16–27 indicates some work towards Level 4 with many areas to be addressed
Less than 16 would indicate a child working at Level 3 or below

Level 5 marking for Test 3
In order to find out how well the child has achieved across Number and Algebra, Shape, Space and Measure and Handling Data at Level 5, add up the three scores in the boxes N5, S5 and H5.

37 upwards indicates a child working well at Level 5
22–36 indicates a child working within Level 4 and towards Level 5
10–21 indicates some work towards Level 5 with many areas to be addressed
Less than 10 would indicate a child working at Level 4 or below

Marking across Levels in Number and Algebra in Test 3
In order to find out how well the child has achieved within Number and Algebra at Levels 3, 4 and 5 add up the three scores in the boxes N3, N4 and N5.

76 upwards indicates a child working well at Level 5
49–75 indicates a child working within Level 4
24–48 indicates a poor Level 4 or Level 3 with many areas to be addressed
Less than 24 would indicate a child working at Level 3 or below

Marking across Levels in Shape, Space and Measure in Test 3
In order to find out how well the child has achieved within Shape, Space and Measure at Levels 3, 4 and 5 add up the three scores in the boxes S3, S4 and S5.

25 upwards indicates a child working well at Level 5
15–24 indicates a child working within Level 4
6–14 indicates a poor Level 4 or Level 3 with many areas to be addressed
Less than 6 would indicate a child working at Level 3 or below

Marking across Levels in Handling Data in Test 3
In order to find out how well the child has achieved within Handling Data at Levels 3, 4 and 5 add up the three scores in the boxes H3, H4 and H5.

26 upwards indicates a child working well at Level 5
17–25 indicates a child working within Level 4
8–16 indicates a poor Level 4 or Level 3 with many areas to be addressed
Less than 8 would indicate a child working at Level 3 or below

Overall Level for Test 3
If you wish an overall Level score, total the child's scores throughout the test by adding all nine boxes.

120 upwards in a probable Level 5
79–119 is a probable Level 4
39–78 is a probable Level 3
Below 39 means the child could be anywhere within the band Levels 1 and 2, depending upon their score.

Answers

Page 12 **1. a.** James **b.** Alice **c.** Alice **d.** Hashim **e.** 203 **f.** James and Hashim
2. a. 236, 263, 326, 362 **b.** Three hundred and sixty two **c.** 623 and 632 **d.** 360 **e.** 300

Page 13 **1.**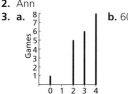
2. a. 26 **b.** 28 **c.** Year 3 **d.** 69 **e.** 108
3. 8, 12, 20, 24, 36

Page 14 **1. a.** 106 **b.** 23 **c.** 32
2. a. ✔ **b.** ✘ **c.** ✔ **d.** ✔ **e.** ✘ **f.** ✔
3. Various shapes may be drawn.

Page 15 **1. a.** ×+ or +× **b.** ×+ **c.** +× **d.** ××
2. a. cube **b.** sphere **c.** tetrahedron or square-based pyramid **d.** cuboid
3. water – litres; weight – grams; length – centimetres

Page 16 **1.** Jane – 60, Billy – 140, Sandeep – 270, Gareth – 800
2. a. 9 **b.** 7 **c.** 7 **d.** 6
3. d is correct
4. a. A (0, 3), B (3, 6), C (6, 3) **b.** (3, 0) **d.** 18 cm²

Page 17 **1. a.** 5 **b.** 7 **c.** 10 **d.** 9
2. a. B **b.** B
3.

Page 18 **1. a.** 144 **b.** 36 **c.** 12.5 **d.** 12.5
2. Ann
3. a. 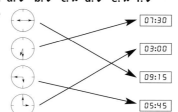 **b.** 60 goals **c.** 3

Page 19 **1. a.** 150 **b.** 200 **c.** 12 **d.** 400
2. a. × 2 + 1 **b.** ÷ 3 + 2
3. a. 294 cm³ **b.** 937.5 cm³

Page 20 **1. a.** 159 **b.** £220
b. Drake up to 14, Murray up to 28, Nelson up to 20
2. a. mode 2 median 2 **b.** mode 5 median 10 **c.** mode 1 median 1

Page 21 **1. a.** £125.00 **b.** £809.00 **c.** £1699.00 **d.** £10 400
2. A = 7.30 m B = 13.53 m C = 9.98 D = 10.75 m
3. 20% of 50 by 1 **b.** 75% of 80 by 20

Page 22 **1. a.** ✘ **b.** ✘ **c.** ✘
2. a. Yes **b.** To the effect that 3.9 is just under 4 and 4 × 4 is 16, so the answer cannot be more than 16.
3. a. finger – 6 cm, coke – 400 g, ant – 3 mm, bucket – 10 l

Page 23 **1. a.** Answers can vary **b.** square **c.** rectangle, square and others **d.** equilateral triangle
2. a. parallelogram
3. octagon

Page 24 **1. a.** 10 **b** 40% **c.** $\frac{8}{40}, \frac{4}{10}, \frac{2}{10}, \frac{1}{5}$ **d.** 80%
2. a. 9 **b** 50 **c.** 37p **d.** 42
3. 59

Page 25 **1. a.** 50 **b.** 25 **c.** 75 **d.** 10 **e.** 40
2. a. 12, 96 **b.** 9, 16, 25 **c.** 5, $2\frac{1}{2}$, $1\frac{1}{4}$ **d.** 10, $\frac{1}{10}$ (0.1)
3. c

Page 26 **1. a.** 445 545 **b.** 128 28
2. a.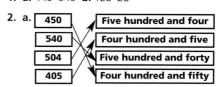
b. 504 **c.** 504 **d.** 504
3. a. 639 **b.** 240 **c.** two hundred and forty

Page 27 **1.** £6.00
2. a. Murray **b.** Drake **c.** Year 3 **d.** 17 **e.** 31
3. 100 ÷ 10 = 10, 16 ÷ 2 = 8, 15 ÷ 3 = 5, 45 ÷ 5 = 9, 2 × 6 = 12, 5 × 4 = 20

Page 28 **1. a.** ✔ **b.** ✔ **c.** ✘ **d.** ✔ **e.** ✘ **f.** ✔
2.
3. a. centimetres **b.** metres **c.** centimetres **d.** metres

Page 29 **1. a.** 71 **b.** 62 **c.** 90 **d.** 81
2. a. equilateral triangle **b.** isosceles triangle **c.** quadrilateral. (Note that the triangles are worth three points each and the quadrilateral is worth one point.)
3. a. 6, 5 **b.** square, rhombus (diamond)

Page 30 **1. a.** A = 8 piles, 90 left over B = 14 piles 27 left over C = 24 piles 6 left over D = 40 piles 29 left over
2. a. 9 **b.** 7 **c.** 7 **d.** 45
3. a. ✔ **b.** ✘ **c.** ✔
4. a. 8 → 1,2,4,8 **b.** 16, → 1,2,4,8,16 **c.** 49 → 1,7,49

Page 31 **1. a.** B and C
2. a. ✔ **b.** ✘ **c.** ✔ **d.** ✘
3. a. Multiply the first two numbers on the top row and then add the third to make the number on the bottom. 21 and 6

Page 32 **1. a.** 90 **b.** 76 **c.** 118 **d.** 54 **e.** 36 **f.** 98
2. a. $\frac{3}{4}$ **b.** $\frac{2}{4}$ or $\frac{1}{2}$ **c.** $\frac{1}{4}$ **d.** $\frac{1}{4}$
3. a. certain **b.** unlikely **c.** likely **d.** even
4. 2

Page 33 **1.** A → (4,0), B → (5,3), C → (3,5), D → (0,4)
2. a. 8 **b.** 30 **c.** 18 **d.** 20
3. 16, 49, 64, 81, 100

Page 34 **1.**

S	1	2	3	4	5	6
F	6	9	8	10	7	10

2. a. £2.25 **b.** 39p **c.** £5500 **d.** £1.64 **e.** £64.50

Page 35 **1. a.** £15 **b.** 4.96 cm **c.** 5.27 m
2. a. $\frac{1}{2} = \frac{15}{30}$ $\frac{2}{3} = \frac{8}{12}$ $\frac{4}{5} = \frac{80}{100}$
3. Asmat – £10.84 Roy – £9.97 Ann – £15.57 Don – £11.62
4. 12

Answers

Page 36
1. **a.** 269 **b.** 147 (marks may be given at discretion)
2. **a.** 60p **b.** 500p or £5.00 **c.** £7.00 **d.** 20
3. 225

Page 37
1. **a.** > **b.** < **c.** > **d.** = **e.** > **f** =
2.

Page 38
1. **a.** 6P is 30, 6M is 28 **b.** 25% **c.** $\frac{1}{3}$ **d.** Mickey Mouse **e.** 17
2. One in two OR 50% OR $\frac{1}{2}$. Previous results do not affect equal outcomes

Page 39
1. d is correct
2.
3. **a.** 13 **b.** 5

Page 40
1. **a.** 820 **b.** 208 or 280 **c.** 208 or 280
2. **a.** 0.6 and 0.05
3. **a.** 10, 100, unit **b.** 280 **c.** 500 **d.** 700 **e.** 497

Page 41
1. d
2. **a.** 9 **b.** pentagons **c.** 3 **d.** 3 **e.** 36 **f.** 6
3. **a.** 1 **b.** 3 **c.** 4 **d.** 2 **e.** 6

Page 42
1. **a.** 6, 9, 5 **b.** 1, 6, 10
2. **a.** 3 **b.** line up to 3 **c.** 19 **d.** $\frac{9}{19}$
3.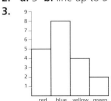
Answers may vary

Page 43
1. **a.** 5 **b.** 5 **c.** 10 **d.** 4
2. **a.** A **b.** I **c.** K **d.** M **e.** S
3. **a.** 16 in l.h. part of circle; 24 in middle; 15 in r.h. part of circle.

Page 44
1. **a.** Aziz –1200, Pete – 4 000, Sue – 12 500, Sophie – 20 800
2. **a.** 72 cm² and 44 cm **b.** 72 cm² and 34 cm **c.** 72 cm² and 36 cm C is correct
3. **a.** 10 **b.** 8 **c.** 9 **d.** 45
4. **a.** 1,2,3,4,6,12 **b.** $3\frac{1}{2}$ (3.5)

Page 45
1. **a.** 6,9,12,15,18,21,24,27 **b.** 3,6,12,24
2. a and e
3. **a.** 80 and 10, 12 and 120
Words to the effect that top two numbers multiplied together makes the bottom number and the top left number is the same as the previous top right.

Page 46
1. **a.** 6.18 **b.** 0.68 **c.** 6.72 **d.** 2.43
2. **a.** £6 **b.** £9.45 **c.** £6.75 **d.** £1.77
3. **a.** 3.7 **b.** 67 **c.** 310

Page 47
1. **a.** 4 **b.** 10
2. 544
3. **a.** 1.45 m **b.** 268 cm **c.** 3.04 m **d.** 470 cm

Page 48
1. **a.** 27 **b.** brown
c.

colour	grey	blue	brown	hazel	green
frequency	9	3	10	3	2

d. (line graph: grey 9, blue 3, brown 10, hazel 3, green 2)

e. $\frac{9}{27}$, $\frac{3}{9}$, or $\frac{1}{3}$

Page 49
1. 1200 ÷ 100 → 12.0
   120 ÷ 1000 → 0.12
   1200 ÷ 10 → 120.0
   120 ÷ 100 → 1.2
2. **a.** 9.8 **b.** 4900, **c.** 1160 **d.** 7600 **e.** 1225 **f.** 1340
3. **a.** 31.68 **b.** 4.26 **c.** 3.15 **d.** 36.5

Page 50
1. **a.** 75 – use discretion if most calculations are correct
b. 1612 – use discretion if most calculations are correct
2. **a.** 24 cm² **b.** 4 cm
3. **a.** A = (B × H) ÷ 2 **b.** 9 cm²

Page 51
1. 1 × 24 2 × 12 3 × 8 4 × 6
2. **a.** A **b.** 7 **c.** $6\frac{1}{2}$ (6.5) **d.** round 6

Page 52
1. **a.** 25° **b.** 8 and 6 **c.** 10° **d.** 4 hours **e.** 9 and 11
2. 4.55

Page 53
1. (diagram of net)
2. **a.** 12 cm³ **b.** 6 cm³
3. **a.** $\frac{150}{750}$, $\frac{15}{75}$, $\frac{1}{5}$ **b.** 80%

Page 54
1. 236, 263, 326, 362
2. **a.** 267 **b.** 340 **c.** 408
3. **a.** 631 **b.** 136
4. **a.** 639 **b.** 240
5. **a.** 10 **b.** 30 **c.** 50 **d.** 60 **e.** 80 **f.** 300 **g.** 700 **h.** 500 **i.** 900

Page 55
1. **a.** £1.76 **b.** £2.14 **c.** £3.50 **d.** £4.89 **e.** £7.40
2. **a.** £1.60 **b.** £1.45 **c.** £2.70 **d.** £3.12
3. **a.** £2.26 **b.** £1.53 **c.** £4.18 **d.** £ 3.50 **e.** £5.06
4. **a.** –3, **b.** –5, **c.** –4, **d.** –2, **e.** –1
5. **a.** £8.40

Page 56
1. 1-c 2-e, 3-d, 4-a, 5-b
2. chicken, ice cream, milk, bread
3. **a.** 0 degrees, –2 degrees **b.** 0 degrees, –5 degrees **c.** 0 degrees, –1 degrees

Page 57
1. e
2. 1 is d, 2 is c, 3 is a, 4 is e, 5 is b
3. **a.** 41 **b.** 33 **c.** 72 **d.** 93 **e.** 77
4. **a.** 63 **b.** 78 **c.** 63p **d.** 45
5. **a.** 75 **b.** 53

Page 58
1. d
2. 1 is d, 2 is b, 3 is e, 4 is c, 5 is a
3. **a.** 26 **b.** 8 **c.** 16 **d.** 38 **e.** 15
4. **a.** 27 **b.** 9 **c.** 41 **d.** 17
5. **a.** 34 **b.** 23

Page 59
1. **a.** 9 **b.** 5 **c.** 2 **d.** 5 **e.** 10 **f.** 10
2. **a.** 15p **b.** 40p **c.** 30p **d.** 20p
3. **a.** 8 **b.** 4 **c.** 7 **d.** 5
4. **a.** 60 **b.** 90 **c.** 40 **d.** 8

Page 60
1. **a.** 12 **b.** 18 **c.** 27 **d.** 21
2. **a.** 3 **b.** 10 **c.** 5 **d.** 8 **e.** 0
3. **a.** 8 **b.** 28 **c.** 20 **d.** 36
4. **a.** 12 **b.** 24 **c.** 32 **d.** 40 **e.** 16
5. **a.** 10 × 4 = 40, 3 × 4 = 12, 40 + 12 = 52
b. 10 × 4 = 40, 5 × 4 = 20, 40 + 20 = 60
c. 10 × 4 = 40, 8 × 4 = 32, 40 + 32 = 72

Page 61
1. **a.** 3r1 **b.** 5r1 **c.** 7r1 **d.** 8r1 **e.** 10r1
2. **a.** 3r4 **b.** 5r1 **c.** 7r3 **d.** 9r2 **e.** 10r3
3. **a.** 2 and 6 **b.** 4 and 7 **c.** 6 and 2 **d.** 8 and 9 **e.** 10 and 5
4. **a.** 6r1 **b.** 6r3 **c.** 8r1 **d.** 1r6 **e.** 7r8
5. **a.** 4r1 **b.** 8r4 **c.** 3r9 **d.** 9r2 **e.** 8r2

Answers

Page 62
1. a. 1r1 b. 2r2 c. 3r2 d. 4r1 e. 5r2
2. a. 3r2 b. 1r2 c. 2r1 d. 6 e. 4r2
3. a. 2r1 b. 5r1 c. 2r2 d. 4r1 e. 5r3
4. a. 3r1 b. 4r2 c. 5r2 d. 4r3 e. 5r2
5. 5

Page 63
1. a. 26 + 47 = b. 32 − 14 = c. 6 × 5 =
   d. 10 × 8 = e. 32 ÷ 4 =
2. a. + b. 3 c. ÷ d. 3 e. 3
3. a. 13p b. 140p (£1.40) c. 69 d. 250 e. 47

Page 64
1. a. 85 b. 82 c. 90
2. 27 and 26
3. 1 + c = 68, 2 + a = 64, 3 + b = 61, 4 + d = 68
4. a. Yes b. 3p left over

Page 65
1. a. 18 b. 26 c. 25 d. 59
2. 37
3. 36
4. a. 30 b. 38 c. 18 d. 13
5. 57

Page 66
1. a. 60 b. 140 c. 270 d. 650
2. a. 200 b. 500 c. 1200 d. 2300 e. 4000
3. a. 3 b. 7 c. 20 d. 35 e. 87
4. a. 4 b. 9 c. 12 d. 25 e. 60
5. a. × 100 b. ÷ 10 c. × 100 d. × 10 e. ÷ 100

Page 67
1. a. 99 b. 69 c. 92 d. 88
2. a. 68 b. 65 c. 93 d. 101 e. 101
3. a. 1 is d, 2 is a, 3 is e, 4 is b, 5 is c
4. Amber
5. £52

Page 68
1. red 58, yellow 76, green 49, pink 67
2. a. 36 b. 32 c. 17 d. 26 e. 37
3. 1 is c, 2 is e, 3 is a, 4 is b, 5 is d
4. 21p
5. 50

Page 69
1. a. 40 b. 72 c. 56 d. 48 e. 64
2. a. 70 b. 28 c. 56 d. 42 e. 63
3. e.
4. a. 7 b. 4 c. 9 d. 10 e. 0
5. a. 7 b. 2 c. 9 d. 3 e. 8

Page 70
1. a. 6 b. 10 c. 7 d. 9 e. 8
2. a. 9 b. 5 c. 8 d. 10 e. 16
3. a. 6r4 or $6\frac{4}{9}$ b. 8r5 or $8\frac{5}{9}$ c. 8r4 or $8\frac{4}{7}$
   d. 9r3 or $9\frac{3}{4}$ e. 16
4. a. $7\frac{3}{6}$ or $7\frac{1}{2}$ b. $8\frac{5}{8}$ c. $8\frac{4}{7}$ d. $9\frac{3}{4}$ e. $10\frac{2}{3}$
5. a. $24\frac{2}{3}$ b. $20\frac{3}{4}$ c. $19\frac{3}{5}$ d. $12\frac{5}{6}$ e. $11\frac{7}{8}$

Page 71
1. Amy £4.24, James £6.27, Alice £6.11, Peter £4.92, Josh £7.10
2. a. 3.21 m b. 3.97 m c. 4.36 m d. 4.32 m e. 1.79 m
3. a. 3.53 b. 5.75 c. 11.44 d. 4.96 e. 5.86
4. d
5. 8.15 m

Page 72
1. £3.04
2. 25 cm or 0.25 m
3. a. 2.62 b. 4.18 c. 0.78 d. 5.19 e. 0.69
4. 1 is d, 2 is a, 3 is e, 4 is c, 5 is b
5. a. 1.18 b. £2.35 c. 2.91

Page 73
1. a. correct b. wrong c. correct d. correct
2. a. 2 b. 6 c. 10 d. 15 e. 18
3. a. 3 b. 5 c. 7 d. 11 e. 20
4. 9
5. $\frac{10}{15}, \frac{2}{3}$
6. 25%, 9 and 3
7. 80
8. 80

Page 74
1. a. 1, 2, 4, 8 b. 1, 2, 3, 4, 6, 12 c. 1, 17
2. 5, 7, 9, 10
3. a. 12, 18, 24 b. 14 c. 24
4. 6, 12, 18, 24, 30
5. 64

Page 75
1. 12 and 18
2. 8 hours
3. a. 20 b. 70 c. 100
4. £2.16
5. 1 medal and 1 badge

Page 76
1. N (2,4) E (4,2) S(2,0) W(0,2)
2. (1, 0), (2,1), (3,2), (4,3), (5,4)
3. A is (2,2) B is (6,3) C is (11,1)
4. E

Page 77
1. a. 2000 b. 10 000 c. 26 000 d. 104 000
   e. 250 000
2. a. 25.0 b. 30.2 c. 114.0 d. 207.0 e. 3626.3
3. a. 130 b. 647 c. 20 d. 1804 e. 3092
4. c and d
5. 230 460 metres

Page 78
1. a. 6 b. 27 c. 50 d. 23 e. 7500
2. 1 is e, 2 is a, 3 is d, 4 is b, 5 is c
3. a. 0.0355 b. 0.816 c. 4.31 67. 823 e. 0.6094
4. a. 6.381 l b. 30.006 l c. 0.847 l d. 21.324 l
   e. 406.004 l
5. 100

Page 79
1. a. Oslo b. Rome, Tokyo, London, Moscow, Oslo
   c. Tokyo and Rome d. Moscow and Oslo
2. a. −4°, −2°, 1°, 3°, 5° b. −10°, −7°, −5°, 0°, 5°
   c. −15°, −10°, 0°, 15°, 20° d. −2°, −1°, 0°, 1°, 4°
   e. −4°, −1°, 1°, 2°, 3°
3. a. 12° b. 4° c. 8° d. 0° e. −4°
4. Moscow 14°, London 14°, Tokyo 13°, Madrid 12°, Quebec 8°

Page 80
1. a. £2.54 b. £3.72 c. £2.90 d. £2.87 e. £4.77
2. e
3. a. 10.6 m b. 3.97 m
4. 3.55 and 4.67

Page 81
1. a. £2.25 b. £1.42 c. £2.84 d. £1.15 e. £2.55
2. 1 is d, 2 is c, 3 is e, 4 is a, 5 is b
3. d
4. a. 2.12 b. 2.56 c. 1.64 d. 1.79 e. 4.38
5. 3.18 m

Page 82
1. Alice – £4.50, James – £5.50, Benedict – £3.60, Katie – £7.05, David – £8.40
2. a. 22.02 b. 33.03 c. 14.68 d. 29.36 e. 25.69
3. a. 7.5 cm b. 3.75 cm c. 2.5 cm d. 1.5 cm
   e. 1.25 cm
4. a. 3.25 b. 12.4 c. 3.75 d. 9.25 e. 64.5
5. 3.25

Page 83
1. James – 6, Alice – 4, Rashid – 8, Larry – 3, 3 left over
2. a. 10 b. 12 c. 15 d. 15 e. 63
3. a. £45 b. £44
4. a. £135 b. £11 500
5. 75% of £300 by £25

Page 84
1. a. 4380 b. 6205 c. 8395 d. 1825 e. 2920
2. a. 3, 6 and 0 b. 1, 9 and 2 c. 35, 90, 82 and 2
   d. 24, 2 and 43 e. 1, 5, 13
3. a. 4176 b. 3900p or 39.00 c. 2160
4. a. 25 942 b. 25 074 c. 24 215 d. 49 704
   e. 14 688
5. 11 201 km

Page 85
1. 19
2. a. 13 b. 35 c. 34 d. 28 e. 13
3. 1 is e, 2 is a, 3 is d, 4 is b, 5 is c
4. a. 14 b. It is correct
5. a. 36 b. 41

Answers

Page 86 1. e
2. **a.** no **b.** no
3. a is correct, b is correct, c is wrong, d is wrong, e is correct
4. **a.** 9 **b.** 6 **c.** 3 **d.** 90 **e.** 31

Page 87 1. c = f + d
2. **a.** 123 cm **b.** 5 cm **c.** 94 cm
3. **a.** 20 **b.** 60 **c.** 7 **d.** 8 **e.** 6
4. 3 × N = 24
5. C = M + P

Page 88 1. **a.** 21 **b.** 39 **c.** 57 **d.** 177 **e.** 297
2. T = (C + W) × 2
3. **a.** 7 **b.** $2\frac{1}{2}$ (2.5) **c.** 14
4. T = (K × 10) ÷ 4

Page 89 1. **a.** square **b.** rectangle (oblong) **c.** triangle **d.** circle **e.** hexagon **f.** pentagon
2.

	Has	Has not
a	✓	
b	✓	
c		✓
d		✓
e		✓
f		✓

3.

Shapes with 1,2,3, or 4 corners	Shapes with more than 4 corners
square	pentagon
rectangle	hexagon
triangle	circle

NOTE: The circle can be considered to have an infinite number of corners

4. Child's choice

Page 90 1. a, c and d
2. a, c and e
3.
(many other choices)
4. b, c and e

Page 91 1. a, c and d
2. (figures)
3. (figures showing letters A, K, T, B, W with lines of symmetry)
4. (figures)

Page 92 1. **a.** b and e
2. (figures)
3. **a.** 4 **b.** 3 **c.** many (infinite) **d.** 6
4. Child's choice

Page 93 1. **a.** cube **b.** cuboid **c.** sphere **d.** cylinder **e.** prism (triangular)
2.

Shapes with flat faces only	Shapes with flat and curved faces
cube	cylinder
cuboid	
prism	

3.

Shapes which can roll	Shapes which cannot roll
sphere	cube
cylinder	cuboid
	prism

4. Child's choice

Page 94 1. **a.** 3 cm **b.** 8 cm **c.** 6 cm **d.** 4 cm
2. **a.** no **b.** no **c.** yes **d.** yes **e.** no
3. **a.** 3 cm **b.** 1 cm **c.** 7 cm **d.** 4 cm
4. **a.** less **b.** less **c.** more **d.** more **e.** more

Page 95 1. **a.** less **b.** more **c.** more or less **d.** less **e.** more
2. **a.** less **b.** more **c.** less **d.** less **e.** more
3. **a.** quarter past one **b.** quarter to five **c.** 10 o'clock

Page 96 1. **a.** ten past six **b.** twenty-five to three **c.** eighteen minutes past nine
2. **a.** quarter past three **b.** half past six **c.** eleven o'clock
3. **a.** 35 minutes **b.** 30 minutes
4. 1 – b, 2 – c, 3 – a

Page 97 1. **a.** no **b.** no **c.** yes
2.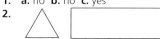
3. pyramid (square based)
4.

other choices are possible

Page 98 1. **a.** congruent **b.** not congruent **c.** congruent
2. **a.** K **b.** C **c.** F **d.** no **e.** no **f.** no
3. Various choices

Page 99 1. **a.** 2 **b.** 3 **c.** 4
2. **a.** 1 **b.** 6 **c.** 4 **d.** 1 **e.** 2 **f.** 4 **g.** many (infinite) **h.** 5 **i.** 2
3. 8

Page 100 1. (figures) **a.** **b.** **c.** **d.**
2. (figures) **a.** **b.** **c.** **d.**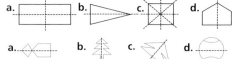
3. **a.** 3 **b.** 7 **c.** 0 **d.** 8 **e.** 1

Page 101 1. **a.** scales – kg **b.** litre jug **c.** tape measure **d.** scales **e.** click wheel **f.** metre ruler
2. **a.** km **b.** litres **c.** g (kg is acceptable) **d.** cm **e.** metres
3. **a.** 100 **b.** 1000 **c.** 1000 **d.** 2

Page 102 1. **a.** 10 cm **b.** 12 cm **c.** 14 cm **d.** 12 cm **e.** 14 cm
2. **a.** 9 cm **b.** $18\frac{1}{2}$ cm **c.** 21 cm **d.** 34 cm
3. **a.** 320 m **b.** 380 cm **c.** 600 cm **d.** 80 cm

Page 103 1. **a.** 2 cm² **b.** 3 cm² **c.** 5 cm² **d.** 9 cm² **3.** 8 cm²
2. **a.** $3\frac{1}{2}$ cm² **b.** 3 cm² **c.** $3\frac{1}{2}$ cm² **d.** 3 cm²
3. **a.** 5 cm² **b.** $7\frac{1}{2}$ cm² **c.** 4 cm² **d.** $6\frac{1}{2}$ cm²

Page 104 1. **a.** 4 cm³ **b.** 8 cm³ **c.** 2 cm³ **d.** 3 cm³
2. **a.** 6 cm³ **b.** 6 cm³ **c.** 5 cm³ **d.** 3 cm³
3. **a.** 7 cm³ **b.** 13 cm³

Page 105 1. **a.** 25° **b.** 60° **c.** 80° **d.** 14°
2. **a.** 110° **b.** 165° **c.** 117° **d.** 172°
3. **a.** acute **b.** obtuse

Page 106 1. **a.** 225° **b.** 260° **c.** 210° **d.** 235°
2. **a.** 300° **b.** 280° **c.** 350° **d.** 305°
3. **a.** 135° **b.** 85° **c.** 260° **d.** 40°

Page 107 1. Child's drawings
2. Child's drawings
3. **a.** AB = 6 cm, BC = 3.5 cm, AC = 5 cm, ∠C = 90°, ∠A = 35°, ∠B = 55°
b. BC = 7 cm, AC = 4 cm, AB = 4 cm, ∠C = 30°, ∠B = 30°, ∠A = 120°
c. BC = 5 cm, AC = 9 cm, AB = 5 cm, ∠A = 25°, ∠B = 130°, ∠C = 25°

Answers

   d. AB = 5 cm, BC = 5 cm, AC = 7 cm, ∠B = 90°, ∠A = 45°, ∠C = 45°

Page 108 **1. a.** a = 110°, b = 70°, c = 110°
   b. a = 30°, b = 150° c = 30°
2. Alternative positions possible
3. a. a = 115°, b = 65°, c = 115°, d = 65° e = 115° f = 65°, g = 115°
   b. a = 130°, b = 50°, c = 130°, d = 130°, e = 50°, f = 50°, g = 130°
4. 180°
5. a. a = 120°, b = 60°, **b.** a = 90°, b = 30°

Page 109 **1. a.** 3 **b.** 4 **c.** lots, many (infinite)
2. a. 3 **b.** 4 **c.** lots, many (infinite)
3. a. 2 **b.** 3 **c.** 4
4. a and b. Alternative correct answers
5. Alternative correct answers

Page 110 **1. a.** 15 cm **b.** 120 cm **c.** just under 3 metres **d.** 10 km
2. a. 180 g **b.** 2 kg **c.** 60 kg
3. a. 2200 ml **b.** 45 l

Page 111 **1. a.** 50 **b.** 35 **c.** 14 **d.** 100 **e.** 86
2. a. 100 **b.** 175 **c.** 310 **d.** 60 **e.** 505
3. a. 1500 **b.** 2200 **c.** 3750
4. a. 3000 **b.** 4500 **c.** 6100 **d.** 7800 **e.** 10 000
5. a. 5000 **b.** 4500 **c.** 2750 **d.** 5200 **e.** 7050
6. a. 4.5 cm **b.** 1.12 m **c.** 3.1 km **d.** 5.75 kg **e.** 8.25 l

Page 112 **1. a.** 3 cm/30 mm **b.** 9 cm/90 mm **c.** 5.5 cm/55 mm **d.** 0.8 cm/8 mm
2. a. silly **b.** sensible **c.** silly **d.** sensible **e.** silly
3. All answers can vary

Page 113 **1. a.** Vijay **b.** James **c.** David **d.** 3 **e.** David
2. a. Katie **b.** Suman **c.** 3 **d.** 2 **e.** David

Page 114 **1. a.** James **b.** Katie **c.** 4 **d.** Bacon **e.** 1
2. a. Vijay **b.** James **c.** David and Alice **d.** maths **e.** Vijay

Page 115 **1. a.** £1.30 **b.** £1.05 **c.** 50p **d.** milk and butter
2. a. 12 **b.** pentagon **c.** square and triangle
3. a. geography **b.** maths and English **c.** 1 hour 30 minutes **d.** 50 minutes

Page 116

Page 117 **1. a.** 2 **b.** chess **c.** ludo **d.** 4 **e.** 14
2. a. 4 **b.** 3 **c.** Lars **d.** 2 **e.** 1

Page 118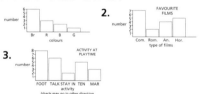

Page 119 **1. a.** 6 **b.** pizza **c.** 1 **d.** fish
2. a. cola **b.** water **c.** 2 **d.** 8

Page 120 **1. a.** Sid **b.** Ann and Kate **c.** Jools **d.** 1 **e.** 27
2. a. Disneyland **b.** Wales **c.** 2 **d.** 4 **e.** 23

Page 121 **1.**

Number on Dice	Frequency
1	3
2	6
3	6
4	5
5	5
6	5

2.

0	9
1	9
2	12
3	3
4	6
5	0
6	0
7	1

3.

1p	7
2p	6
5p	5
10p	5
20p	1
50p	1

4

r	4
b	20
x	6

Page 122 **1.** 2 is 6, 3 is 5, 4 is 4, 5 is 2, 6 is 1. Mode is 2
2. a. 1 **b.** $\frac{1}{2}$ **c.** 0.75 **d.** 50%
3. a. 0 **b.** e **c.** 10p
4. a. 5 and 6 **b.** 1 **c.** $\frac{1}{4}$ and $\frac{1}{2}$ **d.** blue and white

Page 123 **1.** 1, 2, 3, 5, 7, 8, 9 median is 5
   a. 4 **b.** 6 **c.** 6 **d.** 10
2. a. $\frac{1}{2}$ **b.** 42 **c.** 50 **d.** 1
3. a. $6\frac{1}{2}$ **b.** $4\frac{1}{2}$ **c.** $\frac{1}{2}$ **d.** 40 **e.** 18 **f.** 55

Page 124 **1. a.** 1 **b.** 13 **c.** 7 **d.** 24
2. Groupings may vary, e.g.

0–10	11–20	21–30	31–40	41–50
5	7	18	11	9

Page 125 **1.**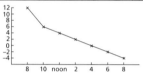
2. a. 4500 (approx.) **b.** 7000 points **c.** 1500
3. a. certain **b.** unlikely **c.** impossible **d.** fair chance

Page 126 **1. a.** 7 **b.** 7 **c.** 6 **d.** 10 **e.** 15p **f.** 6p **g.** 35p **h.** 30p
2. a. 3 **b.** 6 **c.** 10 **d.** 25 **e.** £12.50 **f.** 8 m
3. a. 30 **b.** 12
4. Ben
5. a. 8 **b.** Team A

Page 127 **1. a.** 20° **b.** 15° –24° (9°) **c.** 2
2. a. 26 **b.** 17–41 (24) **c.** 4
3. a. A – 7, B – 8 **b.** B **c.** A – 6 – 8, B – 7 – 9 **d.** $7\frac{1}{2}$ (7.5) **e.** round 5

Page 128 **1. a.** chocolate **b.** 7 **c.** 21
2. a. $\frac{1}{4}$ **b.** $\frac{1}{8}$ **c.** 8 **d.** 4 **e.** blue and red
3. 4

Test 1

1 Four children played a computer game and these are their scores:

James	146	Alice	251
Hashim	180	Roy	212

a. Who had the lowest score? _____

b. Who had the highest score? _____

c. Whose score is an odd number? _____

d. Whose score is in the 10 times table? _____

Dennis played the game later on and had a score of two hundred and three.

e. Write Dennis' score in numbers. _____

f. Which children did Dennis' score beat? _____

2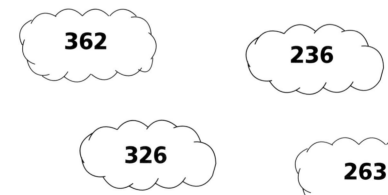

a. Write the numbers in order with the smallest first. _____

b. Write the highest number in words. _____

c. Two more numbers can be made using the digits 2 3 6.

What are the other two numbers? _____ and _____

d. What is 362 to the nearest 10? _____

e. What is 263 to the nearest 100? _____

Test 1

1 Put a ✗ at −3 on this line.

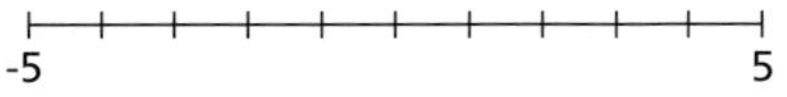

```
├─┼─┼─┼─┼─┼─┼─┼─┼─┼─┤
-5                  5
```

2 This chart shows the number of children in the school with different eye colours.

	Hazel	Grey	Blue
Year 3	24	35	19
Year 4	30	26	14
Year 5	26	28	15
Year 6	28	32	12

a. How many children in Year 4 had grey eyes? _____

b. How many children in Year 6 had hazel eyes? _____

c. Which year group has 19 children with blue eyes? _____

d. How many children are there in Year 5? _____

e. How many children have hazel eyes? _____

3 Circle the numbers which are multiples of 4.

20

14

24

36

12

8

Level 3

N3

H3

N3

TOTAL

Level 3

Test 1

1. Write in the missing numbers.

    a. 75 + 99 + ☐ = 280

    b. 30 + 49 + ☐ = 102

    c. 55 + ☐ + 29 = 116

2. Some shapes have reflective symmetry. Put a tick (✔) in the column if the shape has reflective symmetry and a cross (✘) if it doesn't.

	Shape	✔ or ✘
a.	(rectangle)	
b.	(scalene triangle)	
c.	(bullet/leaf shape)	
d.	(pentagon)	
e.	(irregular trapezium)	
f.	(circle)	

3. Draw a shape of your own which has reflective symmetry.

Test 1

Level 3

1 Billy has used a calculator to help him with his sums. These are the sums which Billy did but the ☐+☐ button and the ☐×☐ button have been removed. Put a ☐+☐ or ☐×☐ in the sums to make them correct.

a. 4 ☐ 3 ☐ 2 = 14

b. 5 ☐ 10 ☐ 6 = 56

c. 10 ☐ 3 ☐ 4 = 52

d. 3 ☐ 4 ☐ 5 = 60

N3
4

2 Write the names of these 3D shapes.

tetrahedron

sphere

cuboid

cube

square based pyramid

Clue	Shape name
a. I have six square faces and right angles at each vertices.	
b. I have one curved surface and no edges.	
c. I have eight edges and am made of four equilateral triangles and one square.	
d. I have 12 edges, two square faces and four rectangle faces.	

S3
9

3 On the left are three different items, and on the right are the units you would use to measure them, but they are mixed up. Match them up by drawing a line from the item on the left to the correct unit for measuring it on the right.

water in a bucket   grams

weight of a cake   centimetres

length of a pencil   litres

S3
3

TOTAL

Level 4

Test 1

1. Football cards come in packs of 10. How many cards does each child buy?

Jane buys 6 packs _____ cards

Billy buys 14 packs _____ cards

Sandeep buys 27 packs _____ cards

Gareth buys 80 packs _____ cards

2. Fill in the numbers in the squares to make each sum correct:

a. 6 × ☐ = 54

b. ☐ × 8 = 56

c. 9 × ☐ = 63

d. 7 × ☐ = 42

3. Only one of these sums is correct. Tick (✔) the sum which is correct.

a. 27
   × 6
   ―――
   142 ☐

b. 49
   × 8
   ―――
   384 ☐

c. 36
   × 7
   ―――
   242 ☐

d. 88
   × 9
   ―――
   792 ☐

4.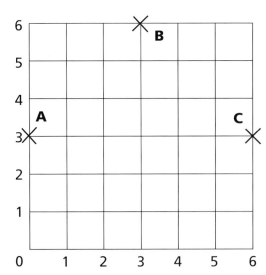

A, B and C are three corners of a square.

a. What are the co-ordinates of

A _____

B _____

C _____

b. Put the fourth corner of the square on the grid and label it **D**.

c. Draw the square.

d. What is the area of the square? _____

Test 1

1 $\boxed{4} \times \boxed{4} = 16$ and $\boxed{2} \times \boxed{2} = 4$

The same number in each sum is missing. Write down the number in these sums.

a. $\square \times \square = 25$ b. $\square \times \square = 49$

c. $\square \times \square = 100$ d. $\square \times \square = 81$

2   a. Only one of these shapes can be cut out and folded to make a cube. Which one? _____

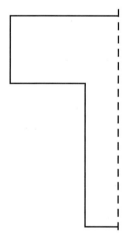
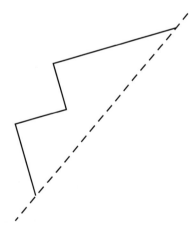
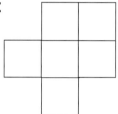

A   B   C

b. Which shape has the longest perimeter? _____

3 Use a mirror or tracing paper to complete these pictures.

a.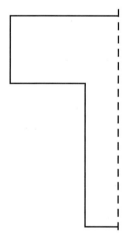

b.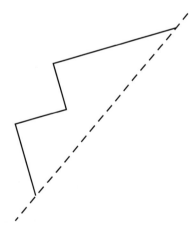

c.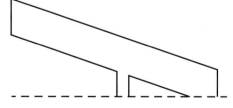

d.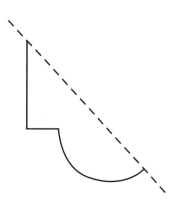

Level 4

N4
4

S4
2

S4
3

TOTAL
Level 4

Level 4 — Test 1

1. Rahmir has collected 240 stamps.

  a. 60% are from India. How many is that? _____

  b. 15% are from England. How many is that? _____

  c. Thirty stamps are from the USA. What percentage is that?
  _____

  d. What percentage is left? _____

2. Four children estimate the length of the school mini-bus.

Put a tick in the box by the most sensible estimate

  Patrick – 40 cm ☐   **Ann – 4 metres** ☐

  Don – 140 cm ☐   **Sue – 40 metres** ☐

3. The school netball team played 20 games in a season and these are the number of goals scored.

number of games	number of goals
1	0
0	1
5	2
6	3
8	4

  a. Draw a bar line graph to show the information.

  b. How many goals were scored in the season?
  _____

  c. What was the mean number of goals scored?
  _____

Test 1

1
  a. 15 000 is the same as how many hundreds? _____

  b. 2000 is the same as how many tens? _____

  c. How many pounds are the same as 120 ten pences? _____

  d. Drawing pins are packed in boxes of 100. How many boxes would be needed to pack 40 000 drawing pins? _____

2 How are these number machines changing the numbers going IN to the numbers coming OUT?

a.
IN → | 3 → 7 | → OUT
     | 5 → 11 |
     | 9 → 19 |
     | 12 → 25 |

answer _____

b.
IN → | 3 → 3 | → OUT
     | 9 → 5 |
     | 15 → 7 |
     | 30 → 12 |

answer _____

3 Work out the volume of each box.

a. _____

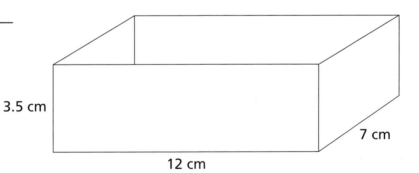

3.5 cm
12 cm
7 cm

b. _____

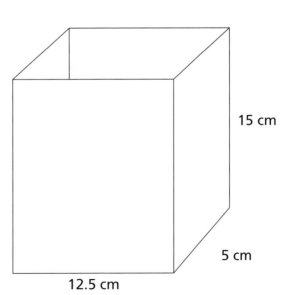

15 cm
12.5 cm
5 cm

Level 4

N4
4

N4
2

S4
2

Level 4

Test 1

1 This bar chart shows how many fish were caught over four days.

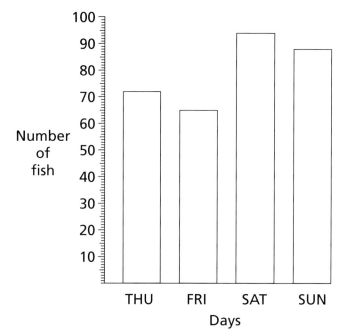

Number of fish caught on four different days.

a. Estimate how many fish were caught altogether on Friday and Saturday.

b. The fish caught on Sunday were sold at £2.50 each and the money was given to charity. How much was given to charity?

2 What is the mode and median in each row?

a. 2, 1, 3, 4, 2, 1, 3, 2, 2   mode _____ median _____

b. 10, 5, 15, 5, 5, 10, 10, 15, 5   mode _____ median _____

c. 1, 0, 1, 1, 1, 0, 1, 0   mode _____ median _____

Test 1

Level 5

1 These items cost this much:

CDs	cassettes	DVDs	video
£12.50	£8.09	£16.99	£10.40

Work out the cost of

a. Ten CDs _____

b. One hundred cassettes _____

c. One hundred DVDs _____

d. One thousand videos _____

2 A builder lays four paths of these lengths:

A 4.62 m **B** 10.85 m **C** 7.30 m **D** 8.07 m

He then adds an extra 2.68 m on to each path.
Now how long will each path be?

A _____ B _____ C _____ D _____

3 a. Which is the larger out of 'one-third of 27' or '20% of 50' and by how much?

_____

b. Which is smaller out of 'one-fifth of 400' or '75% of 80' and by how much?

_____

TOTAL

Level 5

Test 1

1 Help the teacher by marking these sums for her. Put a tick (✔) if they are right and a (✘) if they are wrong.

a.	267	b.	419	c.	342
×	14	×	27	×	36
	1068		2933		20520
+	2670	+	838	+	10260
	3638 ☐		3771 ☐		30780 ☐

2 a. A child thinks that 3.9 × 3.9 is closer to 16 than 17. Is she correct?

_____

b. Explain how you made a decision about part **a**. _____

_____

_____

3 Join up the measurements on the left with a sensible estimate on the right.

3 km

Length of a finger   400g

3 mm

Weight of a can of coke   200 ml

10 l

Length of an ant   6 m

4 kg

Capacity of a fire bucket   6 cm

2 l

TOTAL

Test 1

Level 5

1 a. In box **A**, draw a quadrilateral which has no lines of symmetry.

   b. In box **B**, draw a quadrilateral which has four lines of symmetry.

A.

B.

   c. In box **C**, draw a quadrilateral which has rotational symmetry.

   d. In box **D**, draw a triangle which has rotational symmetry order 3.

C.

D.

2 Write down the name of a quadrilateral which has no lines of symmetry and rotational symmetry order 2.

_____

3 Name a shape with rotational symmetry order 8.

_____

S5 / 8

S5 / 1

S5 / 1

TOTAL

Level 5 — Test 1

1. This pie chart shows the colours of teachers' cars in the car park at Horndean Junior School.

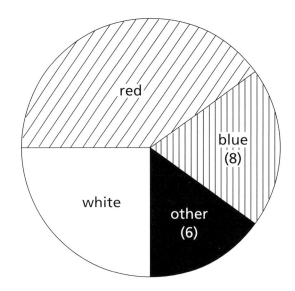

There are 40 cars in the car park.

  a. 25% of the cars are white. How many is that? _____

  b. What percentage of the cars are red? _____

  c. What fraction of the cars are blue? _____

  d. What percentage of the cars are not blue? _____

2. Work out the mean of each row of numbers.

  a. 3, 8, 16 _____

  b. 10, 40, 70, 80 _____

  c. 5p, 10p, 20p, 50p, £1.00 _____

  d. 24, 35, 18, 92, 47, 26, 54, 40 _____

3. The average of four numbers is 67. Three of the numbers are 48, 79 and 82. What is the fourth number?

_____

Test 1

1 Write each of these fractions as a percentage.

a. $\frac{1}{2}$ = _____ %   b. $\frac{1}{4}$ = _____ %   c. $\frac{3}{4}$ = _____ %

d. $\frac{1}{10}$ = _____ %   e. $\frac{2}{5}$ = _____ %

2 Complete each sequence of numbers by putting the correct number in each square.

a. 3   6   ☐   24   48   ☐

b. 1   4   ☐   ☐   ☐   36

c. 40   20   10   ☐   ☐   ☐

d. 1000   100   ☐   1   ☐

3 One of these shapes has an area of 10 cm² and a perimeter of 15 cm. Which one?

a.

4 cm across, $3\frac{1}{2}$ cm

b. 2 cm wide, 5 cm tall

c.
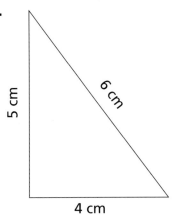
5 cm, 6 cm, 4 cm

Answer _____

Level 5

N5 5

N5 4

S5 1

TOTAL

Test 2

1 Write the missing numbers in each sequence.

a. 145   245   345   ?   ?

b. 428   328   228   ?   ?

2 a. Match the numbers in figures on the left with the numbers in words on the right.

450	Five hundred and four
540	Four hundred and five
504	Five hundred and forty
405	Four hundred and fifty

b. Which of the numbers is nearest to 500? _____

c. Which of the numbers is 500 to the nearest 100? _____

d. Which of the numbers is not in the 5 times table? _____

3   639   567   240

a. Which of the numbers is larger than 567? _____

b. Which of the numbers is less than 567? _____

c. Write 240 in words. _____

Test 2

1 How much did David spend altogether after buying these things? _____

Washing powder   £2.45

Toothpaste   £1.15

Deodorant   £2.40

2 These are the number of house points gained in one week.

	Chichester	Drake	Murray	Nelson
Year 3	25	42	31	40
Year 4	54	23	67	12
Year 5	31	29	26	36
Year 6	44	21	53	22

a. Which house had the highest points in Year 4? _____

b. Which house had the lowest score in Year 6? _____

c. Which year had the highest score in Nelson? _____

d. How many more points did Drake get than Chichester in Year 3? _____

e. How many more points did Murray get than Nelson in Year 6? _____

3 Join up the sum on the left with the answers on the right.

100 ÷ 10 =   9

16 ÷ 2 =   5

15 ÷ 3 =   20

45 ÷ 5 =   8

2 × 6 =   10

5 × 4 =   12

Test 2

1 Put a tick (✔) if the number sentence is true or a (✘) if the number sentence is false.

  a. 14 > 8

  b. 20 = 2 × 10

  c. 19 < 3 × 5

  d. 86 > 68

  e. 35 = 3 × 10

  f. 105 < 110

2 Join up the clocks on the left with the clocks on the right which say the same times.

    07:30

    03:00

    09:15

    05:45

3 Write either 'centimetre' or 'metre' in the gaps so that the sentences will make sense.

  a. My hand is about 10 _____ long.

  b. The classroom is $4\frac{1}{2}$ _____ long.

  c. The child is 120 _____ tall.

  d. The football pitch is 45 _____ wide.

Test 2

1 Replace the letters with numbers to complete this number square.

+	54	45
17	a	b
36	c	d

2 Join the shape to its name.

a.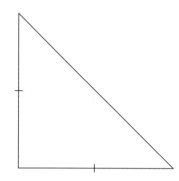

b. 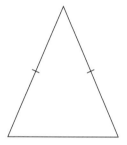   quadrilateral

c. 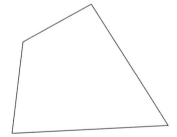   isosceles triangle

equilateral triangle

3 A triangle can be made by putting three matchsticks together.

a. How many matchsticks would be needed to make

a HEXAGON _____

a PENTAGON _____.

b. Two different shapes can be made using 4 matches. What are they?

_____

Test 2

1 Bricks are stacked in piles of 100
How many piles are there at each building site?

How many are left over?

Building site **A**   890 bricks = _____ piles

Building site **B**   1427 bricks = _____ piles

Building site **C**   2406 bricks = _____ piles

Building site **D**   4029 bricks = _____ piles

2 Fill in the numbers in the squares to make each sum correct:

a. 81 ÷ ☐ = 9   b. 49 ÷ ☐ = 7

c. 42 ÷ 6 = ☐   d. ☐ ÷ 5 = 9

3 Peter gets 15 correct spellings out of 20. Read the sentences and put a tick (✔) if it is correct or a cross (✘) if it is wrong.

a. Peter got $\frac{3}{4}$ correct ☐

b. Peter got less than 50% correct ☐

c. Peter got 25% wrong ☐

4 The factors of 6 are 1, 2, 3, and 6.
Write down all the factors of each number.

a. 8 → ☐ ☐ ☐ ☐

b. 16 → ☐ ☐ ☐ ☐ ☐

c. 49 → ☐ ☐ ☐

Test 2

1 Samantha has three pieces of wood. Piece A is 1.34 m, Piece B is 1.27 m, Piece C is 1.26 m. She needs to put two pieces together to make a length of 2.53 m. Which pieces should she use?

_____

2 Billy is not sure what a mirror line is and has drawn the other half of these shapes where he thinks they should be. Put a tick (✔) if he is right or a cross (✘) if he is wrong.

a.

b.

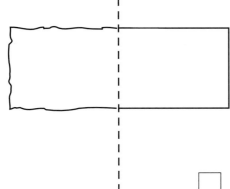

c.

d.

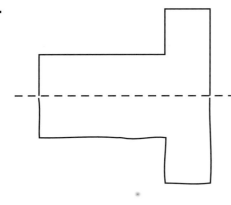

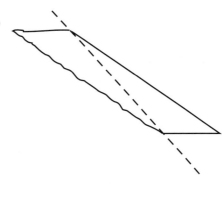

3 Work out how the number in each bottom square has been found and then complete the patterns in the next two boxes.

2	3	1		2	4	3		3	5	2		4	4	5		3	4	
	7				11				17								18	

Test 2

1 Double each of the following numbers.

  a. 45

  b. 38

  c. 59

  d. 27

  e 18

  f. 49

2 What fraction of each of these shapes has been shaded in:

  a. _____

  b. _____

  c. _____

  d. _____

3 Choose one of these statements to go with each sentence.

  likely   unlikely   even   certain

  a. A baby will want feeding. _____

  b. A bull will run away if you chase it. _____

  c. You will need clean socks tomorrow. _____

  d. The next person to walk in the door will be female. _____

4 What is the mode of this group: _____

  2,   5,   1,   3,   2,   4,   5,   2,   3

Test 2

1 Look at this group of co-ordinates.

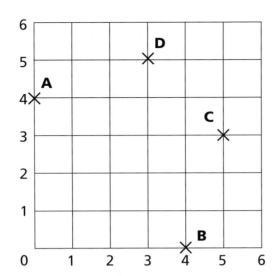

Join up the letters on the left with the co-ordinates on the right.

A	**(4, 0)**
B	**(5, 3)**
C	**(3, 5)**
D	**(0, 4)**

2 Work out the answers to each of these.

a. $\frac{2}{5}$ of 20 _____   b. 15% of 200 _____

c. $\frac{2}{3}$ of 27 _____   d. 40% of 50 _____

3 Write down the square of each of these numbers:

    4   7   8   9   10

_____   _____   _____   _____   _____

Test 2

1 A dice is thrown 50 times and these are the results of each throw.

2	3	4	1	1	5	6	3	2	4
6	4	3	1	2	4	5	2	3	3
4	4	5	3	2	2	6	6	1	4
4	6	2	6	5	2	5	3	1	5
1	4	6	6	6	4	6	5	3	2

Complete this frequency table to show how often each score comes up. (You may draw on the scores if it helps.)

Score	1	2	3	4	5	6
Frequency						

2 Write half of each amount.

a.  £4.50

b.  78 pence

c.  £11,000

d.  £3.28

e.  £129.00

Test 2

1 a. 10 children share £150. How much do they each receive?

___

b. A piece of material 496 cm long is divided into 100 sections. How long is each section?

___

c. A work surface is 5270 mm long. How long is that in metres?

___

2 Join the fraction on the left to the equivalent fraction on the right.

$\frac{1}{2}$ $\frac{80}{100}$

$\frac{2}{3}$ $\frac{8}{12}$

$\frac{4}{5}$ $\frac{15}{30}$

3 Four children start off with these amounts of money:

Asmat – £13.27   **Roy – £12.40**

Ann – £18.00   **Don – £14.05**

They each spend £2.43 on a train ride. How much do they each have left?

Asmat _____ Roy _____ Ann _____ Don _____

4 There are 30 children in a class and 60% are boys. How many are girls?

___

Level 5

Test 2

1 Work out each division sum and show how you find the answer:

a. 34) 9 1 4 6

b. 4 1 1 6 ÷ 2 8

2 t = total cost
n = number of items bought
p = price of each item

So **t = n × p**

a. What will the total cost be if 4 marbles are bought at 15p each?

_____

b. What will the total cost be if 10 lollies are bought at 50p each?

_____

c. If the total cost is £28.00 and 4 items are bought, what is the cost of each item?

_____

d. If the total cost is £200 and each item costs £10, how many items have been bought?

_____

3 The area (**A**) of a square is found by multiplying the length (**L**) of one side, by itself or **A = L × L**. What is the area of a square if its side is 15 cm?

_____

Test 2

Level 5

1 Use the signs = > or < to make each of these sentences true.

   a. A mile is _____ a kilometre

   b. A litre is _____ a gallon

   c. An inch is _____ a centimetre

   d. 10 mm is _____ a centimetre

   e. 1 litre is _____ a pint

   f. 1000 g is _____ a kilogram

S5

2 Draw the net for a square-based pyramid where the sides of the pyramid base are each 4 cm and the faces are equilateral triangles.

S5

TOTAL

Test 2

1 Children in two classes did a survey of their most popular cartoon characters. These pie charts show the results.

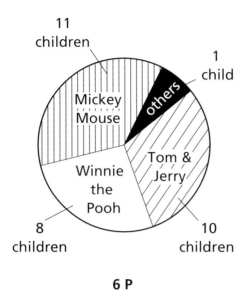
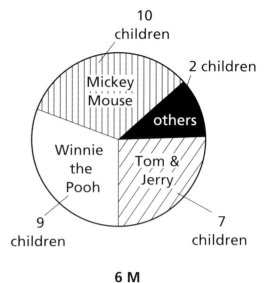

6 P   6 M

a. How many children are there in each class? _____

b. What percentage of children in 6M liked Tom and Jerry? _____

c. What fraction of children in 6P liked Tom and Jerry? _____

d. Which was the favourite programme in 6P? _____

e. How many votes did Winnie the Pooh get altogether? _____

2 An ordinary 2p coin is thrown ten times and lands 'heads' every time. What are the chances it will land 'heads' on the eleventh throw? Explain your answer.

_____
_____
_____
_____
_____
_____
_____
_____
_____

Test 2

1. Put a tick (✔) alongside the sum which gives the answer 4·26.

    a.   3·19
        + 1·17

    b.   6·29
        − 1·03

    c.   1·82
        ×   3

    d. 3)¯12·78

2. Show where you would place each sentence on this probability line:

impossible   fair chance   certain

    A. I'll have to do work at school

    B. I will travel in time back to last week

    C. I'll ride in a car tomorrow

    D. It will be dark tonight

3.
    a. I take 3 away from a number and then divide it by 2. The result is 5. What was the starting number?

    b. I add 4 to a number and then multiply it by itself. The result is 81. What was the starting number?

Test 3

1 Here are three digits:

2   0   8

    a. Use the three digits to make a number which is more than 802.

    _____

    b. Use the three digits to make a number which is less than 802.

    _____

    c. Now use the three digits to make a different number which is less than 802.

    _____

2 Circle the two numbers which add up to 0.65.

0.3   0.6   0.5   0.05   6.0   3.5

3 Each of these numbers has a 7 in it.

    a. What is the 7 worth in each number?

    278 ☐   **735** ☐   **497** ☐

    b. What is 278 to the nearest 10? _____

    c. What is 497 to the nearest 100? _____

    d. What is 735 to the nearest 100? _____

    e. If you arrange the numbers in order with the smallest first, which number is in the middle?

    _____

Test 3

1 Hasan is told by his teacher that one of these sums is wrong. Use a calculator and work out which one.

a. £ 2.40
   + £ 1.72
   ———
   £ 4.12 ☐

b. £ 5.20
   − £ 3.60
   ———
   £ 1.60 ☐

c. £ 1.70
   − £ 0.90
   ———
   £ 0.80 ☐

d. £ 1.65
   + £ 3.47
   ———
   £ 4.02 ☐

2 This graph shows the number of matchsticks Anna uses to make shapes.

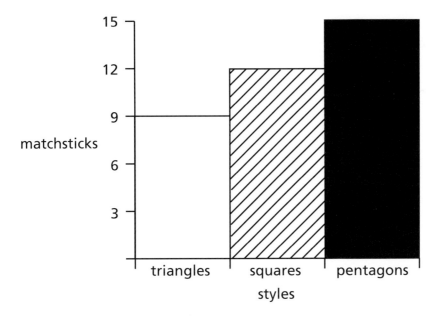

a. How many matchsticks were used to make triangles? _____

b. Which shape had the most matchsticks? _____

c. How many squares did Anna make? _____

d. How many pentagons did Anna make? _____

e. How many matchsticks did Anna use altogether? _____

f. How many hexagons could Anna make if she used all of the matchsticks?

_____

3 Write the remainders only.

a. 25 ÷ 3 _____   b. 31 ÷ 4 _____   c. 5)54 _____

d. 3)32 _____   e. 96 ÷ 10 _____

Level 3

N3
1

H3
6

N3
5

TOTAL

Level 3

Test 3

1 a. Three of these numbers add up to 20. Put a circle around the three numbers.

6   7   9   5

b. Three of these numbers add up to 17. Put a circle around the three numbers.

1   2   6   7   10

2 This graph shows how children in class 6M go to school.

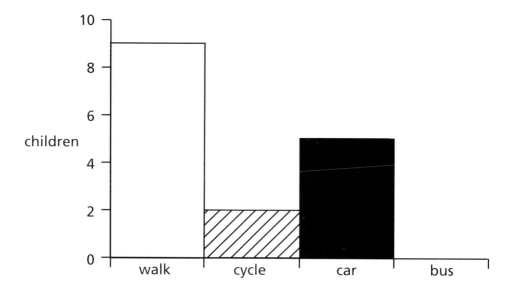

a. How many more children go by car than cycle? _____

b. Three children go by bus. Draw the bar on the graph to show this information.

c. How many children are there in the class altogether? _____

d. What fraction of the class walks to school? _____

3 Draw your own bar chart in the space to show this information.

Favourite colours

red, blue, yellow, blue, blue,

green, blue, red, yellow, blue,

red, blue, yellow, red, blue, blue,

green, yellow, blue, red

42

Test 3

1 What were each of these numbers divided by to give the answers?

a. ☐) 17   3 r 2

b. ☐) 29   5 r 4

c. ☐) 87   8 r 7

d. ☐) 18   4 r 2

2 Use a mirror to help you.
Emmie has been told that four of these capital letters have reflective symmetry but one does not. Draw mirror lines on the letters and help her find out which shape does not reflect.

a. A   b. I   c. K

d. M   e. S

3 Write each of these numbers in its correct place on this diagram.

24   **16**   **15**

multiples of 4 (12 | 18) multiples of 3

Level 4

Test 3

1 There are 100 matches in each box. Some children need matches to make models. How many matches will each child have?

Aziz buys 12 boxes _____ matches

Pete buys 40 boxes _____ matches

Sue buys 125 boxes _____ matches

Sophie buys 208 boxes _____ matches

2 Amy wants to make a model which has a base area of 72 cm² and a perimeter of 36 cm.

a. 4 cm / 18 cm

Area = _____   Perimeter = _____

b. 8 cm / 9 cm

Area = _____   Perimeter = _____

c. 12 cm / 6 cm

Area = _____   Perimeter = _____

Which of these shapes would be correct? _____

3 Fill in the numbers in the squares to make each sum correct:-

a. ☐ × 9 = 90   b. ☐ × 6 = 48   c. 63 ÷ ☐ = 7   d. ☐ ÷ 9 = 5

4 a. Write down all the factors of 12 in order starting with the smallest.

_____

_____

b. What is the median of the numbers? _____

44

Test 3

1 **a.** Write down the multiples of 3 up to 30

| 3 | ☐ | ☐ | ☐ | ☐ | ☐ | ☐ | ☐ | ☐ | 30 |

  b. Which factors of 24 are also multiples of 3?

☐ ☐ ☐ ☐

2 Only two of the shapes on this grid are congruent.

Which ones? _____ and _____.

3 Write in the missing numbers in the next two circles to continue the patterns.

- Circle 1: 2 | 4 / 8
- Circle 2: 4 | 6 / 24
- Circle 3: 6 | 8 / 48
- Circle 4: 8 | 10 / __
- Circle 5: __ | __ / __

Explain how you worked out what the missing numbers were.

_____

_____

_____

_____

Level 4

N4 — 2
S4 — 1
N4 — 5

TOTAL

Level 4

Test 3

1. Work out the answers.

a. 3.51
  + 2.67
  _____

b. 2.43
  − 1.75
  _____

c. 4.03
  + 2.69
  _____

d. 3.21
  − 0.78
  _____

2. These are the normal costs of 4 toys

doll – £8.00   train – £12.60

game – £9.00   model plane – £2.36

In a sale, each toy is sold at 25% off the normal price. How much does each toy cost?

doll _____   train _____

game _____   model _____

3. Estimate what amount is shown on each scale?

a. (LITRES dial, scale 0–5, arrow pointing near 4)

b. (Kg scale 0–100, arrow pointing near 70)

c. millilitres (scale 200–500, arrow at about 300)

Test 3

1   **a.** Sarah thinks of a number, doubles it and then adds 1. Her final number is 9.

What number did she start with? _____

b. Leela thinks of a number, multiplies it by 3 then takes away 1. The final number is 29.

What number did she start with? _____

2 Calculate $\frac{4}{5}$ of 680.

3   **a.** 145 cm is the same as how many metres?

_____

b. 2.68 m is the same as how many centimetres?

_____

c. 304 cm is the same as how many metres?

_____

d. 4.7 m is the same as how many centimetres?

_____

Level 4

Test 3

1 A class did a survey of their eye colours. These are the results of each child:

grey, blue, brown, hazel, brown, brown, grey, brown, green, grey, grey, grey, hazel, brown, brown, grey, grey, hazel, blue, brown, brown, blue, grey, green, brown, brown, grey

a. How many children were in the survey? _____

b. Which was the modal colour? _____

c. Complete this frequency table to show the results.

colour	
frequency	

d. Draw a simple line graph to show the results.

e. What fraction of the class had grey eyes? _____

Test 3

Level 5

1 Match up the sum on the left with the answer on the right by drawing lines between them.

1200 ÷ 100	**0.12**
120 ÷ 1000	**1.2**
1200 ÷ 10	**12.0**
120 ÷ 100	**120.0**

N5 / 4

2 Answer the following questions.

    a. Double 4.9 = ☐

    b. 70 × 70 = ? ☐

    c. 580 × 2 = ? ☐

    d. Double 3800 = ☐

    e. 35 × 35 = ☐

    f. Double 670 = ☐

N5 / 4

3 Work out each sum

    a.   3 · 9 6
       ×   8
       ―――

    b. 38·34 ÷ 9 = ☐

    c.   0 · 4 5
       ×   7
       ―――

    d. 438 ÷ 12 = ☐

N5 / 8

TOTAL

Level 5　　　　　　　　　　　　　　**Test 3**

1　a. A number is multiplied by 49 and the result is 3675.

　　　What was the starting number? _____

　　b. A number is divided by 26 and the result is 62.

　　　What was the starting number? _____

2 The area of a rectangle (**A**) is found by multiplying the length (**L**) by the width (**W**), or

$$A = L \times W$$

　　a. If the length is 6 cm and the width is 4 cm.

　　　What is the area? _____

　　b. If the area is 40 cm² and the length is 10 cm.

　　　What is the width? _____

3 The area (**A**) of a triangle is found by multiplying the base (**B**) by the height (**H**) and dividing by 2.

　　a. Write this out in a formula _____

　　b. What is the area of a triangle with base 7.5 cm and height 2.4 cm?

Test 3

Level 5

1 The area of a rectangle is 24 square cm. What are the possible lengths of its sides? Use whole numbers only.

a [ ]

b [ ]

c [ ]

d [ ]

2 These are the scores of two quiz times in a contest of six rounds.

	R1	R2	R3	R4	R5	R6
A	9	10	4	6	6	7
B	8	7	10	5	6	3

a. Which team had the highest total? _____

b. What was the mean score of team A? _____

c. What was the mean score of team B? _____

d. Which round had the lowest mean score? _____

Level 5

Test 3

1 This graph shows the temperature in a classroom during the school day.

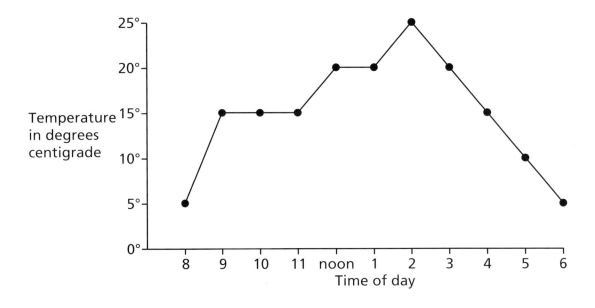

a. What was the highest temperature during the day?

_____

b. At what two times was the room coldest?

_____

c. How much did the temperature rise between 8 and 9 o'clock?

_____

d. How long did it take for the temperature to drop from 25° to 5°?

_____

e. Between which two times did the temperature stay at 15°C?

_____

2 Calculate 7.4 – 2.85.

Test 3

Level 5

1 This is part of a net for a triangular prism. Finish the net accurately using pencil and ruler.

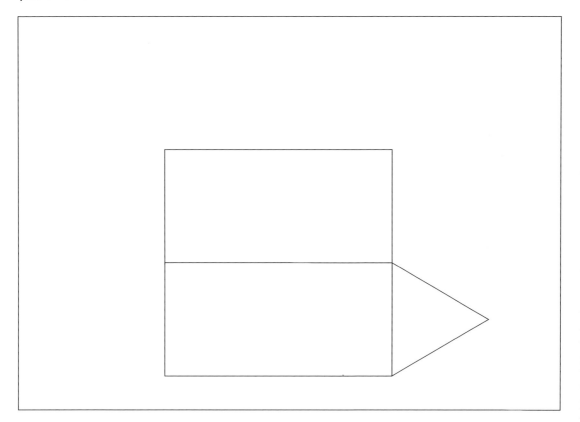

2 Find the volume of each shape

a.

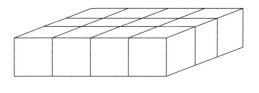

b.

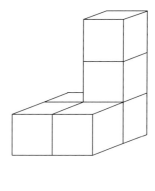

_____   _____

3 750 people attend a school play
150 are old age pensioners

    a. What fraction are old age pensioners? _____

    b. What percentage are not old age pensioners? _____

S5 / 3

S5 / 2

N5 / 2

TOTAL

Level 3

Number and Algebra

Place value up to 1000 approximations

1. 362   236   326   263

Write the numbers in order with the smallest first:

_____

2. a. Write two hundred and sixty-seven using numbers: _____

b. Write three hundred and forty using numbers: _____

c. Write four hundred and eight using numbers: _____

3. The number 163 can be made using the three cards.

[6] [1] [3]

a. Write down the largest number which can be made using the three cards: _____

b. Write down the smallest number which can be made using the three cards: _____

4. 639   567   240

a. Which of these numbers is more than 567? _____

b. Which of these numbers is less than 567? _____

5. 18 to the nearest whole 10 is 20.
Write down what each of these numbers is to the nearest 10.

a. 7 ____   b. 32 ____   c. 46 ____   d. 61 ____   e. 84 ____

230 to the nearest 100 is 200.
Write down what each of these numbers is to the nearest 100

f. 310 ____   g. 680 ____   h. 490 ____   i. 920 ____

54

Number and Algebra
Beginning decimal notation

1. 135p is the same as £1.35. Write each of these amounts using the pound sign and the point to show the pounds and pennies.

    a. 176p   **b.** 214p   **c.** 350p   **d.** 489p   **e.** 740p

2. Write how much each row of coins adds up to. Write it using the pound sign and the point.

    a. £1 + 50p + 10p

    b. £1 + 20p + 20p + 5p

    c. £1 + £1 + 50p + 20p

    d. £1 + £1 + £1 + 10p + 2p

3. Write each amount of money in numbers using the pound sign and the point.

    a. Two hundred and twenty-six pence

    b. One hundred and fifty-three pence

    c. Four pounds eighteen pence

    d. Three pounds fifty pence

    e. Five pounds and six pence

4. 140 cm is the same as 1.40 m.
Match up the letters on the left with the numbers on the right. Write the answers like this: a – 3.

    a. 165 cm   **1.** 2.03 m

    b. 105 cm   **2.** 1.50 m

    c. 230 cm   **3.** 1.65 m

    d. 150 cm   **4.** 2.30 m

    e. 203 cm   **5.** 1.05m

5. A child is given three lots of money. She is given £2.50, £3.65 and £2.25. Use a calculator to work out how much she was given altogether.

Level 3

TOTAL

Level 3

Number and Algebra

Begin to recognise negative numbers in context

1 Five thermometers show temperature in a greenhouse during a winter day. Match the thermometers with the temperatures. Write the answers like this '1 is C'.

 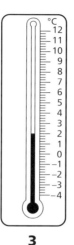 

| 1 | 2 | 3 | 4 | 5 |

a = 0   b = −1   c = 6   d = 2   e = −2

2 These are the temperatures at which some foods should be stored:

bread: 8 degrees   **milk: 4 degrees**

ice cream: −2 degrees   **chicken: −6 degrees (frozen)**

Write the foods in the order of the temperatures at which they should be stored, putting the coldest first.

_____

_____

3 Write the next two temperatures in each sequence.

a. 6 degrees, 4 degrees, 2 degrees, _____, _____

b. 15 degrees, 10 degrees, 5 degrees, _____, _____

c. −3 degrees, −2 degrees, −1 degrees, _____, _____

TOTAL

Number and Algebra

Level 3

Add to 99 using number bonds to 20

1 Jan knows that one of these sums is wrong. Which one is wrong? _____

    a.   3 6   **b.**   2 7   **c.**   4 4   **d.**   3 8   **e.**   5 9
           + 7   + 4   + 9   + 6   + 8
           4 3   3 1   5 3   4 4   6 6

1

2 Match the sums with the correct answers. Write the answers like this: '1 is d'

    1. 32 + 14   _____   **a** = 59

    2. 37 + 12   _____   **b** = 36

    3. 42 + 17   _____   **c** = 49

    4. 45 + 11   _____   **d** = 46

    5. 26 + 10   _____   **e** = 56

5

3 Work out these adding sums and write the answers.

    a.   2 6   **b.**   1 9   **c.**   4 3   **d.**   5 7   **e.**   4 8
           + 1 5   + 1 4   + 2 9   + 3 6   + 2 9

5

4 Write down these sums in the way you like best and work out the answers.

    a. How much is 46 plus 17? _____

    b. Find the total of 26, 17 and 35. _____

    c. Put together 35p and 28p. _____

    d. What is the sum of 14, 15 and 16? _____

4

5   **a.** I take 26 away from a number and I'm left with 49.
         What number did I start with? _____

    b. 35 is taken away from a number and 18 is left.
         What number did we start with? _____

2

TOTAL

Level 3

Number and Algebra

Subtract (99) using number bonds to 20

1. Mitch knows that one of these sums is wrong. Which one is wrong? _____

a.	b.	c.	d.	e.
35	28	67	89	96
− 4	− 3	− 7	− 3	− 6
31	25	60	85	90

2. Match the sums with the correct answers. Write the answers like this – '5 is a'.

1. 23 – 6 _____   **a** = 68

2. 36 – 7 _____   **b** = 29

3. 65 – 8 _____   **c** = 88

4. 97 – 9 _____   **d** = 17

5. 76 – 8 _____   **e** = 57

3. Work out these subtraction sums and write the answers.

a.	b.	c.	d.	e.
43	35	64	73	94
− 17	− 27	− 48	− 35	− 79

4. Write down these sums in the way you like best and work out the answers.

a. What is 42 minus 15? _____

b. What is the difference between 67 and 76? _____

c. Take 39 away from 80. _____

d. Subtract 54 from 71. _____

5. a. I add 46 to a number and end up with 80.
What number did I start with? _____

b. 48 is added to a number and the new number is 71.
What number did we start with? _____

Number and Algebra

Level 3

Use 2, 5 and 10 times tables in whole number problems when multiplying

1 A number is missing in each of these multiplication sums. Write down each sum and put in the missing numbers.

a. 2 × ☐ = 18

b. 5 × ☐ = 25

c. ☐ × 6 = 12

d. ☐ × 9 = 45

e. 7 × ☐ = 70

f. ☐ × 10 = 100

6

2 Each marble costs 5p. How much will each child spend on marbles?

a. Patrick buys 3 marbles _____

b. Gwen buys 8 marbles _____

c. David buys 6 marbles _____

d. Rob buys 4 marbles _____

4

3 Each gobstopper costs 2p. How many gobstoppers does each child buy?

a. Owen spends 16p _____

b. Annie spends 8p _____

c. Joshua spends 14p _____

d. Jessica spends 10p _____

4

4 Erasers come in boxes of 10. How many erasers will there be altogether in:

a. 6 boxes _____

b. 9 boxes _____

c. 4 boxes _____

d. How many boxes will I have if I have 80 erasers? _____

4

TOTAL

Level 3

Number and Algebra

Use 2, 3, 4, 5 and 10 times tables in whole number problems when multiplying

1. Children in a class are given three sweets for each correct answer in a spelling test. How many sweets does each of these children receive:

   a. Tom gets 4 correct. _____
   b. Amy gets 6 correct. _____
   c. Rashid gets 9 correct. _____
   d. Una gets 7 correct. _____

2. What number is missing from each square?

   a. $3 \times \square = 9$
   b. $3 \times \square = 30$
   c. $3 \times \square = 15$
   d. $\square \times 3 = 24$
   e. $\square \times 3 = 0$

3. Football cards are sold in packs of 4. How many cards will each of these children have:

   a. Tamir buys 2 packs. _____
   b. Gary buys 7 packs. _____
   c. Julie buys 5 packs. _____
   d. Suzie buys 9 packs. _____

4. It takes four minutes to build a model. How long will it take to build these numbers of models:

   a. 3 models _____
   b. 6 models _____
   c. 8 models _____
   d. 10 models _____
   e. 4 models _____

5. Daniel works out 16×4 in his head like this:
   First he says that 10×4 is 40
   Then he says that 6×4 is 24
   Then he adds 40 and 24 which makes 64
   So 16×4 is 64

   Work out each of these sums in the same way:

   a. $13 \times 4 = \square$ _____ _____ _____
   b. $15 \times 4 = \square$ _____ _____ _____
   c. $18 \times 4 = \square$ _____ _____ _____

Number and Algebra

Level 3

Use 2, 5, and 10 times tables with whole numbers in dividing with remainders

1 Two flowers are put into each pot. How many pots could be filled and how many would be left over with this number of flowers:

    a. 7 flowers _____ _____   **b.** 11 flowers _____ _____

    c. 15 flowers _____ _____   **d.** 17 flowers _____ _____

    e. 21 flowers _____ _____

2 A worker puts bricks in piles of 5. How many piles could be made with each number of bricks and how many would be left over each time?

    a. 19 bricks _____ _____   **b.** 26 bricks _____ _____

    c. 38 bricks _____ _____   **d.** 47 bricks _____ _____

    e. 53 bricks _____ _____

3 A child is given his pocket money in 10p and 1p coins. How many of each coin does he have if he has these amounts of money:

    a. 26p _____   **b.** 47p _____

    c. 62p _____   **d.** 89p _____

    e. 105p _____

4 Work out each sum and give the remainder if there is one.

    a. $13 \div 2$ **b.** $33 \div 5$ **c.** $41 \div 5$ **d.** $16 \div 10$ **e.** $78 \div 10$

5 Work out each sum and give the remainder if there is one.

    a. $2 \overline{)9}$ **b.** $5 \overline{)44}$ **c.** $10 \overline{)39}$

    d. How many 5s are there in 47 and how many left over?

    e. How many 10s are there in 82 and how many left over?

TOTAL

Level 3

Number and Algebra

Use 3 and 4 times tables with whole numbers in dividing with remainders

1 Triangles can be made by joining three lolly sticks together. How many triangles can be made with each number of sticks and how many will be left over each time?

    a. 4 sticks _____ _____   **b.** 8 sticks _____ _____

    c. 11 sticks _____ _____   **d.** 13 sticks _____ _____

    e. 17 sticks _____ _____

2 4 football cards are put into each pack. How many packs can be made from each number of cards and how many cards will be left over each time?

    a. 14 cards _____ _____   **b.** 6 cards _____ _____

    c. 9 cards _____ _____   **d.** 24 cards _____ _____

    e. 18 cards _____ _____

3 Work out each sum and give the remainder:

    a. $7 \div 3$ **b.** $16 \div 3$ **c.** $10 \div 4$ **d.** $17 \div 4$ **e.** $23 \div 4$

4 Work out each sum and give the remainder:

    a. $3\overline{)10}$ **b.** $3\overline{)14}$ **c.** $3\overline{)17}$ **d.** $4\overline{)19}$ **e.** $4\overline{)22}$

5 A mystery number is less than 10.

3 divides into it with 2 left over.
4 divides into it with 1 left over.

What is the mystery number? _____

TOTAL

Number and Algebra

Level 3

Use calculator methods for four rules

1. If I want to add 13 and 16 on a calculator, I would press the buttons in this order:

[1] [3] [+] [1] [6] [=]

Write down in the same way, the buttons you would press to do each of these sums:

a. 26 add 47 _____

b. 32 take away 14 _____

c. 6 times 5 _____

d. 10 multiplied by 8 _____

e. 32 divided by 4 _____

2. A number or sign has been missed out from each of these calculator sums. Which number or sign is missing each time?

a. [1] [7] [ ] [1] [6] [=] [3] [3]

b. [3] [6] [×] [ ] [=] [1] [0] [8]

c. [2] [8] [ ] [2] [=] [1] [4]

d. [4] [ ] [+] [8] [=] [5] [1]

e. [ ] [2] [−] [1] [3] [=] [1] [9]

3. Use a calculator to work out these problems:

a. A boy is given a 10p and a 20p. He spends 17p of this money. How much does he have left? _____

b. A girl is given 20p for every sum she gets right in a test. If she gets 7 right, how much money will she be given? _____

c. A child has 46 building blocks and is given 35 more. She then looses 12. How many does she have left? _____

d. A boy has 50 stamps and his friend says she has 4 times as many. How many stamps do they have altogether? _____

e. 141 Smarties are shared equally among 3 children. How many do they each receive? _____

Level 3

Number and Algebra

Adding two digit numbers mentally

1 A boy has to add up 37 and 45 in his head. He does it like this.
   First he adds the tens, 30 + 40 is 70
   Then he adds the units, 7 + 5 is 12
   Finally he adds 70 and 12 together = 82

   a. In your head, add together 26 and 59. _____

   b. In your head, add together 44 and 38. _____

   c. In your head, add together 35 and 55. _____

2   (27)   (35)   (26)

Two of these numbers add up to make 53. Which two? _____ _____

3 Which pairs of numbers add up to make answers between 60 and 70?
Write the answers like this 1 + a =

   1. 27   _____   **a.** 29

   2. 35   _____   **b.** 19

   3. 42   _____   **c.** 41

   4. 18   _____   **d.** 50

4 Two children put their money together. One child has 37p, the other has 46p.

   a. Do they have enough money to buy a toy which costs 80p? _____

   b. Do they need more money or would they have money left over? _____

64

Number and Algebra

Subtracting two digit numbers mentally

1 Olaf subtracts 28 from 45 in his head like this:
   First he needs to add 2 to 28 to make 30
   Next he needs to add 10 to 30 to make 40
   Now he needs to add 5 to 40 to make 45
   So altogether he needed 2 + 10 + 5 = 17
   28 away from 45 is 17.

Use Olaf's method to do these subtraction sums

   a. Subtract 14 from 32 _____   **b.** Subtract 27 from 53 _____

   c. Subtract 56 from 81 _____   **d.** Subtract 35 from 94 _____

2 A woman has 61 flowers but 24 die. How many does she have left? _____

3 From 70 peaches, 34 are rotten. How many good peaches are left? _____

4 Choose which number out of these will make the sums correct:

   a. 59 – ☐ = 29   **b.** 64 – ☐ = 26

   c. 45 – ☐ = 27   **d.** 72 – ☐ = 59

5 A box contains 91 pins. 34 are lost when the box is knocked over.

   How many were found? _____

Level 3

4

1

1

4

1

TOTAL

Level 4

Number and Algebra

Multiply and divide whole numbers by 10 and 100

1 Felt tips come in packs of 10. How many felt tips does each child buy?

    a. Billy buys six packs _____   **b.** Jane buys 14 packs _____

    c. Sandeep buys 27 packs _____   **d.** Francois buys 65 packs _____

2 Some children are given money in 1p coins. How many 1p coins does each child have?

    a. Sulu has £2 _____   **b.** Kirk has £5 _____

    c. Uhuru has £12 _____   **d.** McCoy has £23 _____

    e. Bones has £40 _____

3 10 felt tips go into each pack. How many packets would you make from these numbers of felt tips?

    a. 30 felt tips _____   **b.** 70 felt tips _____

    c. 200 felt tips _____   **d.** 350 felt tips _____

    e. 870 felt tips _____

4 Bricks are put into piles of 100. How many piles of bricks could be made out of each lot of bricks?

    a. 400 bricks _____   **b.** 900 bricks _____

    c. 1200 bricks _____   **d.** 2500 bricks _____

    e. 6000 bricks _____

5 Write in either a × sign or a ÷ sign and either 10 or 100 to make each of these sums correct:

    a. 5 ☐ ☐ = 500   **b.** 700 ☐ ☐ = 70

    c. 25 ☐ ☐ = 2500   **d.** 60 ☐ ☐ = 600

    e. 8000 ☐ ☐ = 80

Number and Algebra
Mental and written methods to add to 100

Level 4

1 These are the number of marbles each child has:

Jean Luc – 62   **Worf – 37**
                Riker – 26
Beverly – 55   **Data – 43**

The children add their marbles together in different ways. How many marbles does each pair have?

a. Jean Luc and Worf   b. Riker and Data

c. Worf and Beverly   d. Jean Luc and Riker

4

2 Work out each sum:

a. 47   b. 39   c. 55   d. 43   e. 44
 +21   +26   +38   +58   +57
 ___   ___   ___   ___   ___

5

3 Match up the sums on the left with the answers on the right. Write the answers like this: '1 is a'

1. 54 + 28 _____   a. 81

2. 15 + 66 _____   b. 80

3. 27 + 44 _____   c. 98

4. 32 + 48 _____   d. 82

5. 29 + 69 _____   e. 71

5

4 Five children add up the number of toys they each have. One of them added the list up wrongly. Which one? _____

Corwin	Brand	Oberon	Benedict	Amber
14	19	30	8	32
17	26	25	14	17
32	34	32	46	25
63	79	87	68	84

1

5 A woman has £17 in her purse and then takes £35 out of the bank.

How much does she have altogether? _____

1

TOTAL

Level 4

Number and Algebra

Mental and written methods to subtract to 100

1 Each team has this number of points after a contest:

Red – 76   Yellow – 94   Green – 67   Pink – 85

They each have 18 points taken away because one event did not count.
How many points did each team end up with?

Red _____   Yellow _____   Green _____   Pink _____

2 Work out each sum:

a. 53
   −17
   ____

b. 66
   −34
   ____

c. 44
   −27
   ____

d. 74
   −48
   ____

e. 94
   −57
   ____

3 Match up the sums on the left with the answers on the right. Write the answers like this '1 is a'

1. 31 − 14 _____   a. 58

2. 59 − 31 _____   b. 27

3. 67 − 9 _____   c. 17

4. 50 − 23 _____   d. 16

5. 72 − 56 _____   e. 28

4 A girl has 64p. She spends 25p on sweets and then 18p on a drink.

How much does she have left? _____

5 A fisherman starts off with 92 worms. 24 escape and he uses 18 fishing.

How many worms does he have left? _____

TOTAL

Number and Algebra

Mental and written methods to × up to 10 × 10

Level 4

1 Each copy of a school magazine has 8 pages. How many pages are there altogether in each number of copies?

    a. 5 copies _____
    b. 9 copies _____

    c. 7 copies _____
    d. 6 copies _____

    e. 8 copies _____

2 How many days are there in each number of weeks?

    a. 10 weeks _____
    b. 4 weeks _____

    c. 8 weeks _____
    d. 6 weeks _____

    e. 9 weeks _____

3 Only one of these sums is correct. Which one? _____

a.	b.	c.	d.	e.
6	9	7	5	9
× 8	× 6	× 8	× 9	× 9
46	45	64	35	81

4 What number is missing from each square:

    a. 6 × ☐ = 42
    b. 8 × ☐ = 32
    c. 3 × ☐ = 27

    d. ☐ × 5 = 50
    e. ☐ × 9 = 0

5 The missing numbers in the squares are the same for each question.

Example $\boxed{5} \times \boxed{5} = 25$

What are the missing numbers?

    a. ☐ × ☐ = 49
    b. ☐ × ☐ × ☐ × ☐ = 16

    c. ☐ × ☐ = 81
    d. ☐ × ☐ × ☐ = 27

    e. ☐ × ☐ = 64

TOTAL

Level 4

Number and Algebra

Mental and written methods to divide to 100

1 Alice divides some things into piles of 8. How many things will there be in each pile?

   a. 48 socks _____   b. 80 counters _____

   c. 56 pins _____   d. 72 pennies _____

   e. 64 Smarties _____

2 James is told how many days there are until certain things happen. How many weeks does he have to wait for each thing?

   a. 63 days until his birthday _____

   b. 35 days until the dentist _____

   c. 56 days until a holiday _____

   d. 70 days until the football season _____

   e. 112 days until his sister's wedding _____

3 Ben works out that $20 \div 9$ is 2 with 2 left over. He could write the answer as 2 r 2 or $2\frac{2}{9}$. Write the answers to these sums in both ways.

   a. $58 \div 9$ _____   b. $77 \div 9$ _____

   c. $60 \div 7$ _____   d. $39 \div 4$ _____

   e. $48 \div 3$ _____

4 Do these division sums and give the answers as fractions *not* remainders.

   a. $45 \div 6$ _____   b. $69 \div 8$ _____

   c. $60 \div 7$ _____   d. $39 \div 4$ _____

   e. $32 \div 3$ _____

5 Work out these sums. If they do not work out exactly, give the answers as fractions *not* remainders.

   a. $3\overline{)74}$ _____   b. $4\overline{)83}$ _____

   c. $5\overline{)98}$ _____   d. $6\overline{)77}$ _____

   e. $8\overline{)95}$ _____

Number and Algebra

Add decimals to 2 decimal places

Level 4

1 Five children had these amounts of money:

Amy £1.49   **Peter £2.17**
     Alice £3.36
James £3.52   **Josh £4.35**

They were each given an extra £2.75. How much did they then have?

Amy _____   James _____   Alice _____   Peter _____   Josh _____

2 Floor boards are laid end-to-end. What is the total length of each pair of boards?

a. 1.35 m and 1.86 m _____   b. 3.21 m and 0.76 m _____

c. 2.06 m and 2.3 m _____   d. 1.74 m and 2.58 m _____

e. 0.94 m and 0.85 m _____

3 Work out the total of each sum.

```
a.   1.35     b.   2.53     c.   5.96     d.   1.63     e.   2.64
   +0.46        +1.68        +2.03        +0.78        +1.39
    1.72         1.54         3.45         2.55         1.83
   _____        _____        _____        _____        _____
```

4 One of these sums is wrong. Which one? _____

```
a.  £4.54    b.  £2.05    c.   £8.19    d.  £14.66    e.  £30.10
  + £3.67      + £3.26      + £3.34      + £21.17      + £27.90
    £8.21        £5.31       £11.53       £35.73        £58.00
```

5 A man does the hop, skip and jump.
He hops 2.14 m.
He skips 2.76 m.
He jumps 3.25 m.
How far does he travel altogether? _____

Level 4

Number and Algebra

Subtract to 2 decimal places

1 Donald has £4.50 but gives £1.46 to Pluto.

How much does Donald have left? _____

2 Mickey is 1.63 m tall. Minnie is 1.38 m tall.

How much taller is Mickey than Minnie? _____

3 Write down the answers to these sums.

a.	4.34	b.	5.63	c.	3.45	d.	5.38	e.	2.07
	− 1.72		− 1.45		− 2.67		− 0.19		− 1.38

4 Match up the questions on the left with the answers on the right. Write the answers like this: '1 is a'

1. 2.54 - 1.04 _____ a. 2.18

2. 10.65 - 8.47 _____ b. 4.91

3. 18.25 - 12.74 _____ c. 12.84

4. 26.40 - 13.56 _____ d. 1.5

5. 29.06 - 24.15 _____ e. 5.51

5 a. A piece of wood is 2.67 m long before a 1.49 m section is cut off.

How long is the other piece? _____

b. A child starts off with £5.00 but spends £2.65.

How much does she have left? _____

c. Two numbers add up to 4.57. One of the numbers is 1.66.

What is the other number? _____

Number and Algebra

Approximate proportions, simple fractions and percentages

1 Peter gets 15 correct spellings out of 20
Read these sentences then write whether they are right or wrong.

    a. Peter got $\frac{3}{4}$ correct _____

    b. Peter got less than 50% correct _____

    c. Peter got 25% wrong _____

    d. Peter got more than half right _____

2 Work out 25% of each of these numbers:

    a. 8 _____ **b.** 24 _____ **c.** 40 _____ **d.** 60 _____ **e.** 72 _____

3 Work out $\frac{1}{3}$ of each of these numbers:

    a. 9 _____ **b.** 15 _____ **c.** 21 _____ **d.** 33 _____ **e.** 60 _____

4 A boy looses three-quarters of his marbles. He starts off with 36.

    How many does he end up with? _____

5 A bird lays 15 eggs but 5 do not hatch. What fraction do hatch? _____

6 A pig gives birth to 12 piglets. 75% are male.

    What percentage are female? _____

    How many are there of each? _____

7 A man has 100 stamps but one-fifth ($\frac{1}{5}$) of them have to be sold.

    How many does he have left? _____

8 One-tenth ($\frac{1}{10}$) of a number is 8. What is the number? _____

Number and Algebra

Multiples, factors and squares

1 6 can be exactly divided by 1, 2, 3 and 6. 1, 2, 3 and 6 are called FACTORS of 6.

   a. Write down all of the FACTORS of 8 _____

   b. Write down all of the FACTORS of 12 _____

   c. Write down all of the FACTORS of 17 _____

2 $2 \times 2 = 4$ and $4 \times 4 = 16$
4 and 16 are called SQUARE numbers
Write down which same numbers multiply together to make up these square numbers.

   _____ 25   _____ 49   _____ 81   _____ 100

3 All the numbers in the two times tables are called MULTIPLES of 2.
All the numbers in the three times tables are called MULTIPLES of 3.
So 6 is a MULTIPLE of 2 *and* 3.

   a. Write down the next three numbers after 6 which are multiples of 2 and 3.

   _____   _____   _____

   b. Write down a number between 10 and 15 which is a multiple of 2 and 7.

   _____

   c. Write down the lowest number which is a multiple of 3 and 8.

   _____

4 Write down all of the EVEN numbers which are multiples of 3, up to 31.

   _____

   _____

5 Which square number comes between 60 and 70? _____

Number and Algebra

Level 4

Use simple formulae expressed in words

1 For every black sock a child has, she has two white socks.

If she has 6 black socks, how many white socks does she have? _____

How many socks does she have altogether? _____

2 It takes a girl 2 hours to build a model car. If she builds 3 cars and has an hour off in between each car, how long will she take altogether?

_____

3 In this formula, **n** stands for nuts and **s** stands for squirrels.

n = 10s

This formula means that the number of nuts eaten is 10 times the number of squirrels. How many nuts would be eaten with the following number of squirrels:

    a. 2 squirrels _____   **b.** 7 squirrels _____   **c.** 10 squirrels _____

4 An ice cream costs 60p and a flake costs 12p.

total cost = cost of ice cream + cost of flake

Work out the cost of three ice creams with flakes. _____

5 A badge is given free with every four tokens. A medal is given free with every 5 badges. If a child collects 24 tokens, how many badges and how many medals will he get?

_____

75

Level 4

Number and Algebra

Co-ordinates in first quadrant

1 What are the co-ordinates of the compass points, North, South, East and West?

N _____

E _____

W _____

S _____

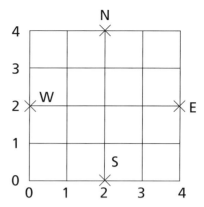

2 Give the co-ordinates of all the points on the straight line.

_____   _____

_____   _____

_____

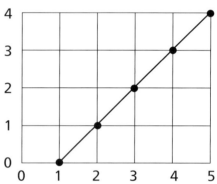

3 What are the co-ordinates of the missing corner of each square?

A _____

B _____

C _____

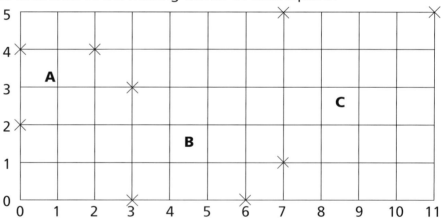

4 Four of these co-ordinates are labelled properly but one is wrong.

Which one? _____

A = $(1, 1\frac{1}{2})$

B = $(2\frac{1}{2}, 4)$

C = $(4\frac{1}{2}, 2)$

D = $(4, 2\frac{1}{2})$

E = $(0, 5\frac{1}{2})$

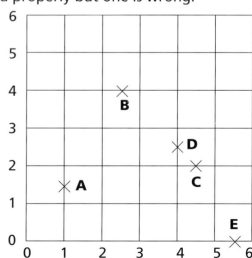

Number and Algebra

Level 5

Multiply whole numbers and decimals by 10, 100 and 1000

1 Sugar cubes come in packs of 1000. How many sugar cubes will there be in each number of packs?

   a. 2 packs _____   b. 10 packs _____   c. 26 packs _____

   d. 104 packs _____   e. 250 packs _____

2 Work out each of these sums:

   a. 2.5   b. 3.02   c. 11.4   d. 20.7   e. 362.63
       × 10   × 10   × 10   × 10   ×   10
       ____   ____   ____   ____   _____

3 These measurements are given in metres. How much are the same distances in centimetres?

   a. 1.3 m _____   b. 6.47 m _____   c. 0.20 m _____

   d. 18.04 m _____   e. 30.92 m _____

4 Three of these sums are correct but two are wrong. Which ones are correct and which ones are wrong?

   a. 4.26 × 1000 = 4260.0 ☐

   b. 10.6 × 1000 = 10 600.0 ☐

   c. 8.03 × 1000 = 803.0 ☐

   d. 267.31 × 1000 = 26 731.0 ☐

   e. 80.94 × 1000 = 80 940.0 ☐

5 A bicycle race is 230.46 km long. How far is this distance in metres?

   _____

Level 5

Number and Algebra

Division of whole numbers and decimals by 10, 100 and 1000

1 There are 1000 metres in a kilometre. Change each of these distances from metres into kilometres.

a. 6000 m _____   b. 27 000 m _____   c. 50 000 m _____

d. 23 000 m _____   e. 7 500 000 m _____

2 Match up each of the sums on the left with the answers on the right. Write the answers like this: '1 is a'

1. 4.6 ÷ 10 = _____   a. 46.0

2. 460.0 ÷ 10 = _____   b. 0.0046

3. 0.46 ÷ 10 = _____   c. 4.6

4. 0.046 ÷ 10 = _____   d. 0.046

5. 46.0 ÷ 10 = _____   e. 0.46

3 Divide each of these numbers by 100.

a. 3.55 _____   b. 81.6 _____   c. 431.0 _____

d. 6782.3 _____   e. 60.94 _____

4 A litre is the same as 1000 ml. Write each of these volumes as l.
EXAMPLE: 3241 ml = 3.241 l

a. 6381 ml _____   b. 30 006 ml _____

c. 847 ml _____   d. 21 324 ml _____

e. 406 004 ml _____

5 What have I divided 53.31 by if I get the answer 0.5331? _____

TOTAL

Number and Algebra

Order, add and subtract negative numbers in context

1 Some children read the temperatures in five cities from the newspapers. These are the temperatures they see:

Rome 10° **Tokyo 7°**

Moscow −2°

Oslo −7° **London 0°**

  a. Which city was the coldest? _____

  b. Write down the cities in order with the warmest first.

  _____ _____ _____

  _____ _____

  c. Which two cities had a difference in temperature of 3 degrees?

  _____ _____

  d. Which two cities had a temperature difference of 5 degrees?

  _____ _____

2 Rearrange each row of temperatures so that the lowest one is first.

  a. 3°, 5°, 1°, −4°, −2° _____ _____ _____ _____ _____

  b. −7°, −10°, −5°, 0°, 5° _____ _____ _____ _____ _____

  c. 15°, 0°, −10°, 20°, −15° _____ _____ _____ _____ _____

  d. 0°, 4°, −1°, 1°, −2° _____ _____ _____ _____ _____

  e. 1°, 2°, 3°, −4°, −1° _____ _____ _____ _____ _____

3 Each of these temperatures is raised by 8 degrees. What will the new temperatures be?

  a. 4° _____   b. −4° _____   c. 0° _____   d. −8° _____   e. −12° _____

4 This chart shows the temperatures of five cities at midday and at midnight. By how many degrees does the temperature change in each of the cities?

CITY	MIDDAY	MIDNIGHT	
MOSCOW	4°	−10°	_____
LONDON	12°	−2°	_____
TOKYO	−1°	−14°	_____
MADRID	17°	5°	_____
QUEBEC	0°	−8°	_____

Level 5

4

5

5

5

TOTAL

Level 5

Number and Algebra

Add with decimals to 2 decimal places

1. These are the amounts of money that five children collected for charity:

James £1.78   **Alice £2.63**

Benedict £0.76

Rosalind £1.09   **Eve £2.14**

Work out how much each of these pairs of children would have raised if they put their money together.

a. James and Benedict _____   b. Alice and Rosalind _____

c. Benedict and Eve _____   d. James and Rosalind _____

e. Alice and Eve _____

2. One of these sums is wrong. Which one? _____

a. 2.46 + 3.92 = 6.38   b. 4.63 + 2.88 = 7.51

c. 5.09 + 3.76 = 8.85   d. 2.66 + 3.47 = 6.13

e. 4.84 + 0.29 = 5.03

3. a. Three floor boards are put end-to-end. They measure 2.4 m, 3.7 m and 4.5 m. What is the total length of the floor boards?

_____

b. Three children measure 1.06 m, 1.24 m and 1.67 m. What is the total height of the children?

_____

4. Two of these numbers add up to 8.22. Which two? _____ _____

a. 5.92   b. 2.28   c. 3.55   d. 1.73   e. 4.67

Number and Algebra

Subtract with decimals to 2 decimal places

1 Take £1.45 away from each of these amounts of money.

   a. £3.70 _____   b. £2.87 _____

   c. £4.29 _____   d. £2.60 _____

   e. £4.00 _____

2 Match up the questions on the left with the answers on the right. Write the answers like this: '1 is a'

   1. 11.36 − 6.39 _____   a. 37.74

   2. 6.07 − 2.88 _____   b. 7.27

   3. 17.32 − 8.43 _____   c. 3.19

   4. 41.00 − 3.26 _____   d. 4.97

   5. 19.50 − 12.23 _____   e. 8.89

3 A carpenter has a piece of wood 1.46m long and needs to add another piece to it to make it 3.72 long.

   Which of these pieces would be the correct length? _____

   a. 1.86 m   b. 2.56 m   c. 1.26 m   d. 2.26 m   e. 1.36 m

4 Work out each of these subtraction sums.

   a. 2.44   b. 3.90   c. 4.21   d. 5.36   e. 8.82
      −0.32   −1.34   −2.57   −3.57   −4.44
      _____   _____   _____   _____   _____

5 A path has to be 10.00 m long but the builder runs out of concrete after 6.82m.

   How much farther does he have to go? _____

Level 5

Number and Algebra

Multiply and divide with decimals to 2 decimal places

1 These are the amounts of money five children have each week.

Alice £1.50   James £2.75   Benedict £1.80   Katie £2.35   David £4.20

Their mother decided to double the amount of pocket money she gave the boys and triple the amount she gave to the girls. How much did they each get after the raise?

_____   _____   _____   _____   _____

2 Multiply 3.67 by each of these numbers:

  a. 6 _____   b. 9 _____   c. 4 _____   d. 8 _____   e. 7 _____

3 Copper piping is 30 cm long. How long will each piece be if it is cut into the following number of pieces:

  a. 4 pieces _____   b. 8 pieces _____

  c. 12 pieces _____   d. 20 pieces _____

  e. 24 pieces _____

4 Work out each of these sums:

  a. 13 ÷ 4 = _____   b. 62 ÷ 5 = _____

  c. 30 ÷ 8 = _____   d. 111 ÷ 12 = _____

  e. 903 ÷ 14 = _____

5 A number is multiplied by 24 and the answer is 78.

What was the number? _____

Number and Algebra

Level 5

Calculate fractional and percentage parts using a calculator

1 A bag contains 24 sweets.
James is given one quarter ($\frac{1}{4}$), Alice is given one sixth ($\frac{1}{6}$), Rashid is given one third ($\frac{1}{3}$) and Larry is given one eighth ($\frac{1}{8}$).
How many sweets do they each get and how many are left over?

_____ _____ _____ _____ _____

2 Work out each of these amounts:

a. $\frac{2}{3}$ of 15 _____   b. $\frac{3}{4}$ of 16 _____

c. $\frac{3}{5}$ of 25 _____   d. $\frac{5}{8}$ of 24 _____

e. $\frac{7}{10}$ of 90 _____

3 Shop A usually sells trainers at £60 but in a sale they are sold at 25% off that price. Shop B usually sells the same trainers at £55 but in a sale they are sold at 20% off that price.

a. How much do the trainers cost at shop A? _____

b. How much do the trainers cost at shop B? _____

4 a. A fridge which usually cost £180 is being sold at 75% of its normal price.

How much is it being sold for? _____

b. A motor car which usually sells for £10000 goes up in price by 15%.

What is the new price? _____

5 A woman is offered either $\frac{5}{6}$ of £240 or 75% of £300.

Which is the most and by how much? _____

Level 5

Number and Algebra

Multiply 3 digit by 2 digit number

1. There are 365 days in a normal year. How many days are there in each of these number of normal years?

  a. 12 years _____   b. 17 years _____

  c. 23 years _____   d. 5 years _____

  e. 8 years _____

2. What are the missing numbers from each of these sums?

```
  a.    2 8 7      b.      4 5 6     c.      3 3 8    d.      8 2 4    e.      2 _ 4
     ×    3 9          ×     2 7          ×     5 4        ×     4 3        ×     2 4
        2 5 8 _          3 _ 9 2          1 _ _ 2          _ _ 7 2          _ 8 _ 6
      8 _ 1 _            _ 1 _ 0        1 6 _ _ 0        3 _ 9 6 0        4 2 8 0
     1 1 1 9 3         1 2 3 1 2        1 _ _ 5 _       3 5 _ _ 2        5 _ _ 6
```

3.

  a. When I divide a number by 24, the answer is 174.

   What is the number? _____

  b. There are 26 children in a class and each child collects 150 pennies for charity.

   How much do they collect altogether? _____

  c. A gardener plants 12 rows of carrots with 180 carrots in each row.

   How many carrots does he plant altogether? _____

4. Work out each of these multiplication sums:

  a. 763 × 34 _____   b. 597 × 42 _____

  c. 835 × 29 _____   d. 654 × 76 _____

  e. 408 × 36 _____

5. A delivery man knows that he travels 487 km each day. He works 23 days a month.

How far does he travel in a month? _____

Number and Algebra

Divide 3 digit by 2 digit number

Level 5

1 17 children share 323 Smarties equally between them. Without using a calculator, work out how many Smarties each child gets.

_____

2 Each of these sums works out exactly. Work out the answer.

a. 247 divided by 19 _____   b. 595 ÷ 17 = _____

c. How many times does 26 go into 884? _____

d. 868 ÷ 31 = _____   e. Divide 63 into 819 _____

3 Match up the questions on the left with the answers on the right. Write the answers like this: '1 is a'

1. 234 ÷ 13 _____   a. 17

2. 289 ÷ 17 _____   b. 29

3. 946 ÷ 86 _____   c. 25

4. 754 ÷ 26 _____   d. 11

5. 850 ÷ 34 _____   e. 18

4
a. I multiply a number by 67 and get the answer 938.

What number did I multiply by? _____

b. Ann is told that 33 multiplied by 24 is 792. Divide 792 by 24 to see if this is correct.

_____

5
a. What is the largest number I can multiply 28 by to give me an answer as close as possible to 1000?

_____

b. I arrange 984 counters in rows of 24. How many are there in each row?

_____

TOTAL

Level 5

Number and Algebra

Check through use of inverse operations

1 One of these answers is wrong. Add the bottom line of each question to the answer line to see which answer is wrong.

a.	37	b.	152	c.	214	d.	601	e.	830
	−19		− 67		−105		−365		−468
	18		85		109		236		352

2 a. A child adds 59 marbles to 86 marbles and thinks the answer is 155.

Is she correct? _____

b. I know that I started with 226 potatoes and ended up with 450. I think I added 324.

Am I correct? _____

3 Daniel has worked out five multiplication sums and knows he can check back to see if they are right by dividing the answer by one of the numbers.
EXAMPLE: 26 × 7 is 182. So 182 ÷ 7 should be 26.
Use the same method to work out if these sums are right or not. Three are right, two are wrong.

a. 69 × 5 = 345 _____   b. 144 × 12 = 1728 _____

c. 34 × 32 = 988 _____   d. 25 × 25 = 500 _____

e. 46 × 53 = 2438 _____

4 Which numbers are missing from the squares in each sum?

a. 5 × ☐ = 45   b. ☐ × 9 = 54

c. 36 ÷ ☐ = 12   d. ☐ ÷ 15 = 6

e. 35 + ☐ = 66

Number and Algebra

Level 5

Construct and express using simple formula with one operation

1 The total cost of a meal is the cost of the food plus the cost of the drink. If we call the cost of the food '**F**' and the cost of the drink '**D**', write a formula for the total cost (**C**) of the meal.

_____

2 In this formula, '**C**' stands for the height of the child and '**S**' stands for the height of her shoes. '**T**' stands for the total height.

$$T = C + S$$

a. If **C** is 120 cm and **S** is 3 cm, what is **T**? _____

b. If **C** is 115 cm and **T** is 120 cm, what is **S**? _____

c. If **S** is 4 cm and **T** is 98 cm, what is **C**? _____

3 In this formula, '**N**' stands for an unknown number. What is the missing number each time?

a. $4 + N = 24$ b. $10 + N = 70$

c. $8 \times N = 56$ d. $\dfrac{48}{N} = 6$

e. $N \times N = 36$

4 A child thinks of a number, multiplies it by 3 and the answer is 24. Write this as a formula using **N** for the missing number.

_____

5 The total cost of a model is the cost of the model (**M**) plus the cost of the postage (**P**). Write a formula which shows how the total cost is worked out.

_____

TOTAL

Level 5

Number and Algebra

Construct and express simple formula using 2 decimal places

1 The formula $\quad\quad\quad\quad N \times 6 - 3$
means multiply any number by 6 then take away 3 to get a new number.
Work out the new number when **N** is:

   a. 4 _____   b. 7 _____   c. 10 _____   d. 30 _____   e. 50 _____

2 The total cost of a bar of chocolate is the cost of the chocolate (**C**), plus the cost of the wrapping (**W**), times 2.
Write down a formula which shows the total cost (**T**) of the bar of chocolate.

_____

3 This formula $\quad\quad\quad\quad (A + B) \div 2 = C$
means that to find **C**, we have to add **A** and **B** together and then divide by 2.
Work out each of the following questions:

   a. If **A** is 5 and **B** is 9, what is **C**? _____

   b. If **A** is 4 and **B** is 1, what is **C**? _____

   c. If **A** is 6 and **C** is 10, what is **B**? _____

4 Four people are going to share the cost of a trip. To find the cost of a trip (**T**) for each person, I have to multiply each kilometre (**K**) by 10p then divide by 4.
Write a formula to show how much each person will have to pay.

_____

Shape, Space and Measures

Classify 2-D shapes

Look at these shapes and then answer the questions.

a.    b.    c.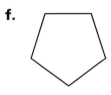

d. 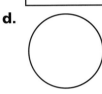   e. 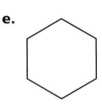   f.

1 Write down the name of each shape.

a. _____   b. _____   c. _____

d. _____   e. _____   f. _____

2 We can classify these shapes by looking at right angles.
Copy this chart and complete it:

	Has right angles	Does not have right angles
a		
b		
c		
d		
e		
f		

3 We can classify the shapes by looking at the numbers of corners.
Copy this chart and complete it:

Shapes with 4 corners or less	Shapes with more than 4 corners

4 Classify the shapes into groups in a way you choose. Explain how you have grouped them.

_____

_____

_____

Level 3

Shape, Space and Measures

Reflective symmetry

1 Three of these shapes have been cut into equal halves by a mirror line.

Which three shapes? _____ _____ _____

a.   b.   c.   d.   e.

2 Three of these capital letters have been cut into equal halves by a mirror line.

Which three capital letters? _____ _____ _____

a. A b. D c. E d. O e. Y

3 Trace these five shapes onto paper and draw a line onto each one which cuts it into two equal pieces.

a.   b. c. d.  e.

4 Use a mirror to help you.
Three of these shapes have been cut into equal halves by a mirror line.

Which three shapes? _____ _____ _____

a.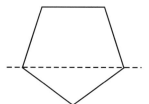

b.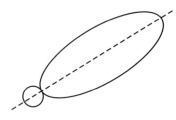

c.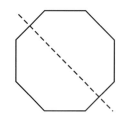

d.

e.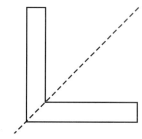

90

Shape, Space and Measures

Reflective symmetry

Use a mirror to help you.

1 Three of these capital letters have been cut into equal halves by a mirror line.

Which three capital letters? _____ _____ _____

a. C   b. H   c. I   d. K   e. S

2 Only one half of each shape has been drawn. Trace the half and then complete the shape by drawing the other half.

a. 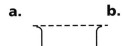   b.   c.   d.   e.

3 Only one half of each capital letter has been drawn. Trace the half and then complete the letter by drawing the other half.

a.   b.   c.   d.    e.

4 Trace these shapes and complete them. The dotted line is the mirror line.

a.   b.   c.   d.   e.

Level 3

Shape, Space and Measures

Reflective symmetry

Use a mirror to help you.

1 Three of these shapes can be cut into halves in more than one way.

Which three shapes? _____ _____ _____

a. ▭   b. 8   c. G   d. N   e. △

2 Each of these shapes has 2 mirror lines. Trace the shape and draw on the mirror lines.

a. ▯   b. H   c. ⌇   d. I   e. ∞

3 How many different mirror lines does each shape have?

a. □   b. △   c. ○   d. ⬡

4 Draw
   a. A capital letter with no symmetry

   b. A capital letter with just one mirror line

   c. A shape with two mirror lines

   d. A number between 0 and 10 with no symmetry

   e. A shape with 5 mirror lines

Shape, Space and Measures

Level 3

Classify 3-D shapes

Look at these shapes and then answer the questions.

a.   b.   c.   d.   e.

1 Write down the correct mathematical name of each shape.

a. _____ b. _____ c. _____ d. _____ e. _____

2 We can classify the shapes by looking at the types of faces they have.
Copy this chart and complete it:

Shapes with flat faces only	Shapes with flat and curved faces

3 We can classify shapes by whether or not they can roll.
Copy this chart and complete it:

Shapes which can roll	Shapes which cannot roll

4 Classify the shapes into groups in a way you choose. Explain how you have grouped them.

_____
_____
_____
_____
_____

Level 3

Shape, Space and Measures

Length and capacity in contexts

1 Estimate how long each of these lines is to the nearest centimetre.

a. ─────────── b. ──────────────────────

c. ────────────────────── d. ─────────

2 Answer YES or NO to whether these sentences are sensible or not.

a. A child's finger is 42 cm long _____

b. A motor car is 95 cm long _____

c. A basketball player is 2 m tall _____

d. A can of cola is 10 cm high _____

e. The distance from England to Australia is 50 km _____

3 Use a ruler to measure these lines to the nearest centimetre.

a. ──────────── b. ────

c. ────────────────────────── d. ──────────

4 Write MORE if you think these things could contain more than 1 litre.
Write LESS if you think these things could contain less than 1 litre.

a. Thimble b. Can of Cola c. Bath

_____ _____ _____

d. Petrol tanker _____ e. Fire bucket _____

Shape, Space and Measures

Mass and time

Level 3

1 Write MORE if you think these things weigh more than 1 g.
Write LESS if you think these things weigh less than 1 g.

a. A flea

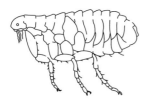

_____

b. A table

_____

c. A drop of water

_____

d. A snow flake

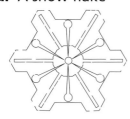

_____

e. A car

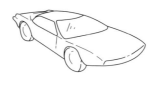

_____

2 Write MORE if you think these things weigh more than 1 kg.
Write LESS if you think these things weigh less than 1 kg.

a. An eraser

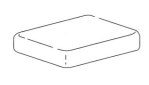

_____

b. A giraffe

_____

c. A calculator

_____

d. A baby's shoe

_____

e. TV set

_____

3 Write the times each of these clock faces says:

a. _____

b. _____

c. _____

5

5

3

TOTAL

Level 3

Shape, Space and Measures

Time

1 Write the time each of these clock faces says:

a. _____ b. _____ c. _____

  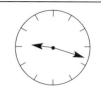

2 Write the time each of these digital clocks says:

a. _____ b. _____ c. _____

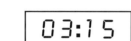 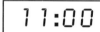

3 How many minutes between each pair of clock faces?

a. and _____

b.  _____

4 Which normal clock face goes with which digital clock?

1. _____ a. 10:50

2. _____ b. 08:30

3. _____ c. 05:07

Shape, Space and Measures

Level 4

3–D models

1 This is the net (plan) for a cube:

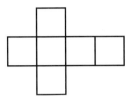

It could be cut out and folded into a cube. Write YES if these nets could be made into cubes and NO if they could not.

a. _____   b. _____   c. _____

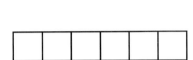 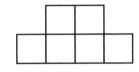 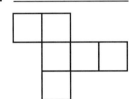

2 These are three parts of a net for a triangular prism.

Draw the other two parts which are needed to finish it.

3 This is a net for a 3-D shape.

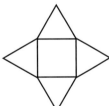

What shape will it be when it is cut out and folded?

_____

4 Draw a net for a box of tissues which looks like this:

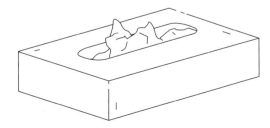

Level 4

Shape, Space and Measures

Common 2-D shapes – congruent shapes

1 Congruent shapes are exactly the same shape and size. Write down if each pair of shapes is CONGRUENT or NOT CONGRUENT.

Pair a

Pair b

Pair c

2 Look at these shapes:

a. Which shape is congruent with **A**? _____

b. Which shape is congruent with **B**? _____

c. Which shape is congruent with **D**? _____

d. Are **E** and **H** congruent? _____

e. Is **G** congruent with anything? _____

f. Are **I** and **J** congruent? _____

3 Draw a shape congruent with **D** and **F** but a different way round.

Shape, Space and Measures

Orders of rotational symmetry

Level 4

1 How many different ways can each shape rotate (turn) to fit into the hole.

a. _____ b. _____ c. _____

 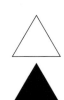

2 The order of rotational symmetry means the number of different ways a shape can fit into its own shape. Write down the order of rotational symmetry for each of these shapes:

a. _____ b. _____ c. _____

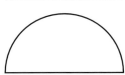 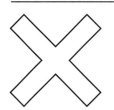

d. _____ e. _____ f. _____

 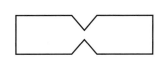 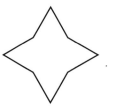

g. _____ h. _____ i. _____

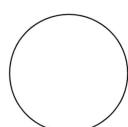 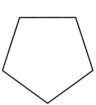 

3 What is the order of rotational symmetry of this shape: _____

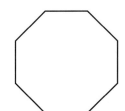

Level 4

Shape, Space and Measures

Reflect in mirror line

1 Trace these shapes and use a mirror to find the mirror lines – the lines of symmetry. Draw on the lines of symmetry.

a.    b.   c.   d.

2 Half of each of these shapes has been drawn, and the line of symmetry for the shape is shown. Trace the shapes and complete them.

a.

b.

c.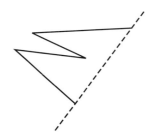

d.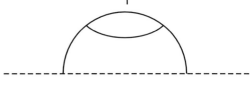

3 Which number is made by reflecting each of these shapes using the mirror line?

a.   b.   c.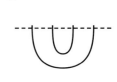

_____   _____   _____

d.    e.

_____   _____

Shape, Space and Measures

Appropriate instrument and accuracy

1 Choose between the following measuring instruments.

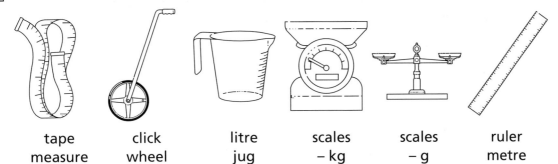

tape measure — click wheel — litre jug — scales – kg — scales – g — ruler metre

What would be the best instrument to measure each of the following:

a. A bag of potatoes _____

b. Some milk _____

c. My waist measurement _____

d. Some marbles _____

e. Length of the playground _____

f. The classroom _____

2 ### grams (g), litres (l), centimetres (cm), metres (m), kilograms (kg), kilometres (km)

What would be the best unit to measure each of the following:

a. The distance between England and France _____

b. The capacity of a car's petrol tank _____

c. The weight of some sugar _____

d. The length of a felt tip pen _____

e. The height of a tree _____

3 a. How many centimetres in a metre? _____

b. How many grams in a kilogram? _____

c. How many metres in a kilometre? _____

d. About how many metres high would a tall person be?

_____

Level 4

6

5

4

TOTAL

Level 4

Shape, Space and Measures

Perimeters of simple shapes

1 Work out the perimeter of each of these shapes:

a. _____
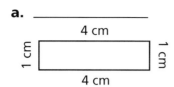

b. _____
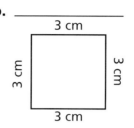

c. _____
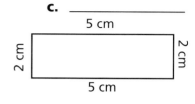

d. _____
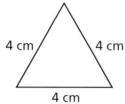

e. _____
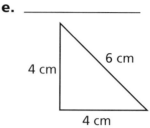

2 Work out the perimeters of each of these shapes:

a. _____
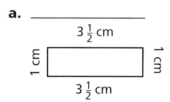

b. _____
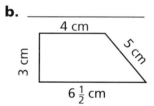

c. _____
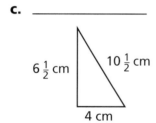

d. _____
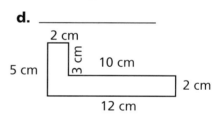

3 Work out the perimeters of each of these things:

a. Football pitch _____
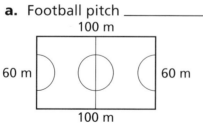

b. _____
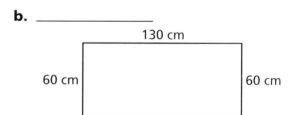

c. Flag _____
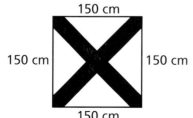

d. Book cover _____
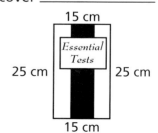

Shape, Space and Measures

Areas by counting squares

1 Find the area of each shape:

a. _____

b. _____

c. _____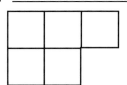

d. _____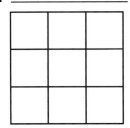

e. _____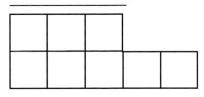

2 Find the area of each shape:

a. _____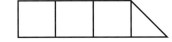

b. _____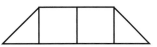

c. _____

d. _____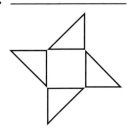

3 Find the area of each shape:

a. _____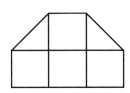

b. _____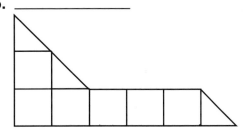

c. _____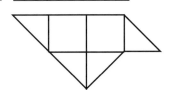

d. _____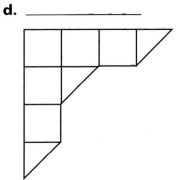

Level 4	**Shape, Space and Measures**

Volume by counting cubes

1 What is the volume of each shape? (count the cubes)

a.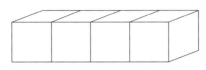

b.

c.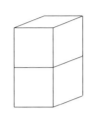

d.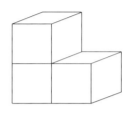

2 What is the volume of each shape?

a.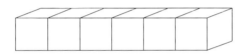

b.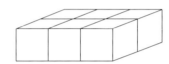

c.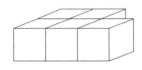

d.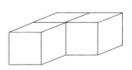

3 What is the volume of each shape?

a.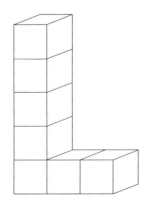

b.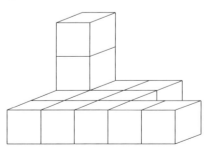

Shape, Space and Measures

Level 5

Measure angles

1 Use a protractor to measure these angles:

a.
_____

b.
_____

c.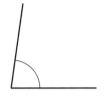
_____

d.
_____

2 Use a protractor to measure these angles:

a.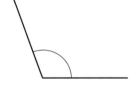
_____

b.
_____

c.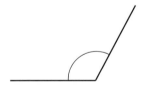
_____

d.
_____

3 What is the mathematical name for

a. An angle between 0° and 90° _____

b. An angle between 90° and 180° _____

TOTAL

Level 5

Shape, Space and Measures

Measure angles

1 Use a protractor to measure these angles.

a.

b.

c.

d.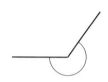

2 Use a protractor to measure these angles:

a.

b.

c.

d.

3 Use a protractor to measure these angles:

a.

b.

c.

d.

Shape, Space and Measures

Draw angles

1 Draw each of these angles.

    a. 25°   **b.** 150°   **c.** 243°   **d.** 327°

2 Draw an equilateral triangle with sides 7 cm long.

3 Measure all the sides and angles of these triangles.

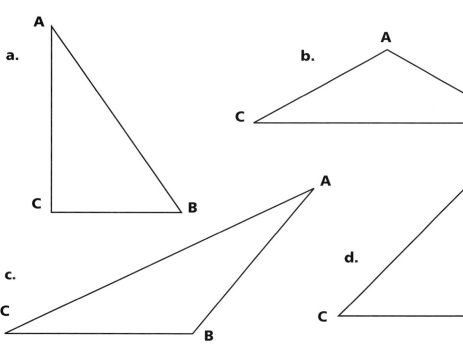

Shape, Space and Measures

Angle language

1 Work out the missing angles where each pair of lines intersect.

a.
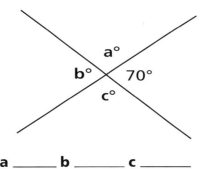

a _____ b _____ c _____

b.
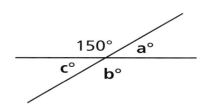

a _____ b _____ c _____

2 Draw two lines 5 cm long which are parallel to each other.

3 Work out the missing angles when a straight line crosses these parallel lines.

a.
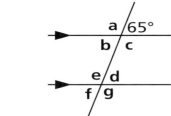

a _____ b _____ c _____ d _____

e _____ f _____ g _____

b.
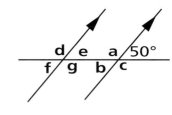

a _____ b _____ c _____ d _____

e _____ f _____ g _____

4 All triangles have the same number of degrees – how many? _____

5 Work out the missing angles in these diagrams.

a.
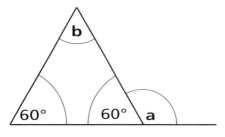

a _____ b _____

b.
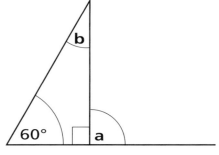

a _____ b _____

Shape, Space and Measures

Symmetry of 2-D shapes

Level 5

1 How many lines of symmetry does each shape have?

a. _____   b. _____   c. _____

  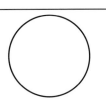

2 What is the order of rotational symmetry of each of the shapes in question 1?

a. _____   b. _____   c. _____

3 What is the order of rotational symmetry of each of these shapes?

a. _____   b. _____   c. _____

 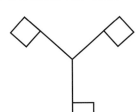 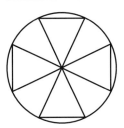

4   **a.** Draw a shape which has 2 lines of symmetry and order of rotation 2.

  b. Draw a shape which has 4 lines of symmetry and order of rotation 4.

5 Draw a shape which has no lines of symmetry and order of rotation 2.

Level 5

Shape, Space and Measures

Imperial/metric units

1 This chart shows old (imperial) measuring units compared with metric ones.

Imperial	Metric
Inch	about $2\frac{1}{2}$ cms
Foot	about 30 cm
Yard	just under a metre
Mile	about $1\frac{2}{3}$ kms

Rewrite these sentences changing the imperial units to metric ones.

a. The pencil is 6 inches long. _____

b. The snake was 4 feet long. _____

c. The room was 3 yards high. _____

d. The journey was 6 miles. _____

2 This chart shows old (imperial) units compared with metric ones.

Imperial	Metric
Ounce	about 30 g
Pound	about $\frac{1}{2}$ kg
Stone	about 6 kg

Rewrite these sentences changing the imperial units to metric ones.

a. The eggs weighed about 6 ounces. _____

b. The cake weighed 4 pounds. _____

c. The woman weighed 10 stone. _____

3 This chart shows old (imperial) units compared with metric ones.

Imperial	Metric
Pint	about 550 ml
Gallon	about $4\frac{1}{2}$ l

Rewrite these sentences changing the imperial units to metric ones.

a. The jug held 4 pints of milk.

_____

b. The car was filled with 10 gallons of petrol.

_____

Shape, Space and Measures

Level 5

Convert one metric unit to another

1 Write each of these lengths in millimetres:

   a. 5 cm _____   **b.** 3.5 cm _____   **c.** 1.4 cm _____

   d. 10 cm _____   **e.** 8.6 cm _____

2 Write each of these lengths in centimetres:

   a. 1.00 m _____   **b.** 1.75 m _____   **c.** 3.10 m _____

   d. 0.60 m _____   **e.** 5.05 m _____

3 Write each of these lengths in metres:

   a. 1.5 km _____   **b.** 2.2 km _____   **c.** 3.75 km _____

4 Change each of these amounts into grams:

   a. 3 kg _____   **b.** 4.5 kg _____   **c.** 6.1 kg _____

   d. 7.8 kg _____   **e.** 10.0 kg _____

5 Change each of these amounts into millilitres:

   a. 5 l _____   **b.** 4.5 l _____   **c.** 2.75 l _____

   d. 5.20 l _____   **e.** 7.05 l _____

6 Add these amounts together:

   a. 3 cm and 15 mm (Answer in cm only) _____

   b. 12 cm and 1 metre (Answer in m only) _____

   c. 2.5 km and 600 m (Answer in km only) _____

   d. 4 kg and 1750 g (Answer in kg only) _____

   e. 2250 ml and 6 l (Answer in l only) _____

TOTAL

Level 5 — Shape, Space and Measures

Sensible estimates

1. Estimate how long each of these lines is (i) to the nearest centimetre, and (ii) to the nearest millimetre.

a. _____   b. _____

(i) _____ (ii) _____   (i) _____ (ii) _____

c. _____   d. ____

(i) _____ (ii) _____   (i) _____ (ii) _____

2. Answer either SILLY or SENSIBLE to each of these sentences.

a. My cereal bowl holds 9 l of milk _____

b. The garden path is 95 cm wide _____

c. My brother weighs 1400 kg _____

d. The washing line is 1000 cm long _____

e. A banana weighs 7 gm _____

3. Make a sensible estimate about each of these things:

a. The weight of a felt tip pen (in g) _____

b. The height of the classroom door (in cm) _____

c. The width of your desk (in cm) _____

d. The weight of your shoe (in g) _____

e. The weight of your teacher's whistle (in g) _____

Handling Data

Level 3

Tables – extract and interpret

1. Look at this table and then answer the questions.

Ages in Years and Months of My Friends

Name	Age
James	8 yrs 10 mths
Alice	7 yrs 6 mths
Vijay	8 yrs 5 mths
David	6 yrs 0 mths
Suman	7 yrs 7 mths
Katie	7 yrs 4 mths

a. Which child is 8 years 5 months old? _____

b. Which child is the oldest? _____

c. Which child is exactly 6 years old? _____

d. How many children are 7 years old? _____

e. Which child is younger than Katie? _____

5

2. Look at this table and then answer the questions.

Favourite Days and Seasons of My Friends

Name	Favourite day	Favourite season
James	Saturday	Summer
Alice	Friday	Summer
Vijay	Saturday	Summer
David	Sunday	Spring
Suman	Friday	Autumn
Katie	Saturday	Winter

a. Which child liked Saturday and Winter best? _____

b. Which child liked Friday and Autumn best? _____

c. How many children liked Summer best? _____

d. How many children liked Saturday best but not Winter? _____

e. Only one child liked Sunday best – who was it? _____

5

TOTAL

Handling Data

Tables – extract and interpret

1 Look at this table and then answer the questions.

What My Friends have For Breakfast

Name	Toast	Cereal	Tea	Coffee	Egg	Porridge	Bacon
Vijay	✔	✔		✔			
Katie		✔	✔		✔		
Suman	✔		✔		✔		
Alice	✔					✔	
James	✔		✔		✔		✔
David	✔		✔		✔		

a. Only one child has bacon – which one? _____

b. Only one child does not have toast – which one? _____

c. How many children have tea? _____

d. What does James have different from David? _____

e. How many children do not have a drink? _____

2 Look at this table and then answer the questions.

Three Favourite Subjects of My Friends

Name	English	Science	Maths	Art	P.E.	History
David	✔	✔	✔			
Katie	✔			✔		✔
Vijay		✔	✔		✔	
James	✔	✔				✔
Alice	✔	✔	✔			
Suman	✔			✔	✔	

a. One child did not like English – which one? _____

b. Which child liked English, Science and History? _____

c. Two children liked exactly the same things –

who were they? _____

d. What did Alice like that James didn't? _____

e. Who liked PE but not Art? _____

Handling Data

Lists – interpret and extract

Level 3

1 Look at this list and then answer the questions.

Item	Cost
Eggs	£1.00 a dozen
Milk	30p a pint
Bread	45p a loaf
Butter	60p a pound

a. How much would a dozen eggs and a pint of milk cost? _____

b. How much would a loaf of bread and a pound of butter cost? _____

c. How much would 6 eggs cost? _____

d. Which two items cost 90p when added together? _____

2 Look at this list and then answer the questions.

Shape	Number of sides
Square	4
Triangle	3
Pentagon	5

a. How many sides do the shapes have altogether? _____

b. Which shape has 2 more sides than a triangle? _____

c. Which two shapes have a total number of sides of 7?

_____ _____

3 Look at this list and then answer the questions.

Subject	Length of homework
Maths	1 hour
English	1 hour
History	30 minutes
Science	30 minutes
Geography	20 minutes

a. Which subject has 20 minutes homework? _____

b. Two subjects have 1 hour homeworks –

which ones? _____ _____

c. How long would a maths and a history homework take? _____

d. How long would a science and geography homework take? _____

TOTAL

Level 3

Handling Data

Construct pictograms

1 Show this information on a pictogram. Use a ☺ to show each child

Children who like types of food

Type of food	Number of children
Chips	5
Ice cream	4
Milk shakes	6
Baked beans	3

2 Show this information on a pictogram. Use a to show each lot of 3 apples

Number of apples each child picks

Child	Apples
John	12
Anne	6
Bill	15
Mary	9

3 Show this information on a pictogram. Use a to show each lot of 5 pizzas.

Number of pizzas eaten in a month.

Child	Pizzas
David	5
Katie	20
Alice	30
James	15

Handling Data

Interpret pictograms

1 Look at this pictogram and then answer the questions.

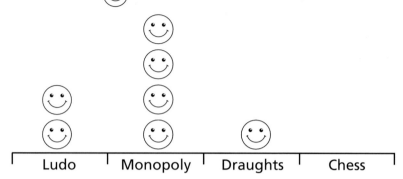

Number of children who like games

Each ☺ means 2 children like a game

a. How many children like draughts? _____

b. Which game does nobody like? _____

c. Four children like one game – which one? _____

d. How many more children like Monopoly than Ludo? _____

e. How many children have said what they have liked? _____

2 Look at this pictogram and then answer the questions.

Number of children who like chocolate bars

Each 🍫 means 2 children

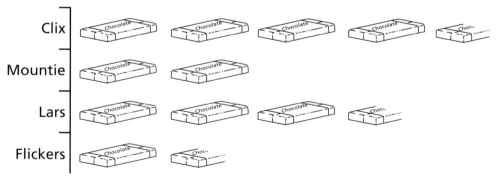

a. How many children like Mounties? _____

b. How many children like Flickers? _____

c. Which chocolate bar is liked by 7 children? _____

d. How many children like Clix more than Lars? _____

e. How many children like Mounties more than Flickers? _____

Level 3

Handling Data

Construct bar charts

1 Show this information on a bar chart

Colour of my friends' hair

Colour	Number
Brown	6
Red	3
Blonde	2
Grey	1

2 Show this information on a bar chart – include a title.
My class voted for their favourite type of film. These are the results:

Type	Number
Comedy	7
Romance	2
Animal	4
Horror	5

3 My friends said what they liked to do best at playtime. These are the results:

8 liked football, 6 liked talking, 2 liked staying in, 5 liked tennis and 3 liked marbles.

Show the information on a bar chart.

Handling Data

Interpret bar charts

1 Look at this bar chart and then answer the questions.

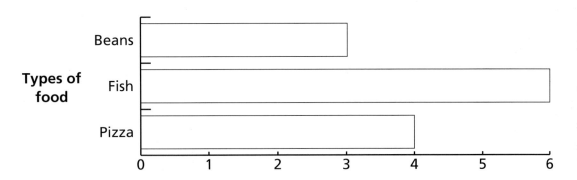

a. How many children liked chips with fish? _____

b. Four children liked which food with chips? _____

c. How many children liked pizza and chips more than beans and chips?

   _____

d. Which was the favourite food with chips? _____

2 Look at this bar chart and then answer the questions.

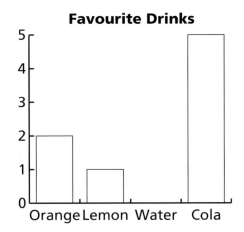

a. Which was the favourite drink? _____

b. No one liked one drink – which was it? _____

c. How many children liked orange? _____

d. How many children were asked altogether? _____

Level 3

Level 3 — Handling Data

Interpret bar charts

1 Look at the bar chart and then answer the questions.

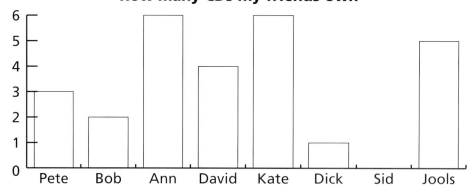

How many CDs my friends own

a. Only one child has no CDs – which one? _____

b. Two children each have 6 CDs – which ones?

_____   _____

c. Which child has five CDs? _____

d. How many more CDs does David have than Pete? _____

e. How many CDs were owned altogether? _____

2 Look at the bar chart and then answer the questions.

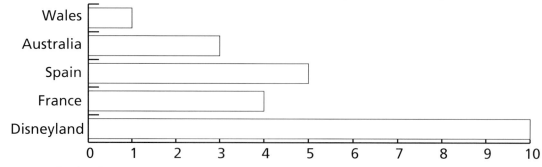

Where my friends would like to go on holiday

a. Which place was the most popular? _____

b. Only one person wanted to go to one country – which one?

_____

c. How many more children wanted to go to Spain than Australia? _____

d. How many children wanted to go to France? _____

e. How many children were asked altogether? _____

Handling Data

Level 4

Collect data and record using frequency table

1 A dice is thrown 30 times and the result recorded:

**4, 2, 6, 5, 4, 2, 5, 1, 3, 6, 5, 2, 4, 6, 5,
3, 3, 3, 6, 1, 4, 2, 5, 3, 4, 2, 6, 2, 1, 3**

Copy this frequency table and complete it using the information above.

Number on Dice	Frequency
1	
2	
3	
4	
5	
6	

2 These are the number of goals scored by 40 teams in a football league:

**2, 1, 0, 4, 1, 2, 1, 4, 0, 0,
3, 2, 0, 4, 7, 2, 4, 2, 1, 0,
1, 0, 2, 3, 2, 2, 1, 1, 4, 2,
0, 2, 1, 4, 3, 2, 0, 0, 2, 1**

Draw a frequency table to show this information.

3 A girl collected these coins in one month.

**2p, 1p, 10p, 2p, 5p, 50p,
20p, 10p, 10p, 2p, 5p, 1p,
2p, 5p, 10p, 5p, 1p, 1p, 1p,
2p, 10p, 5p, 1p, 1p, 2p**

Show this information on a frequency table.

4 A survey was made of hair colour in a class of 32 children. Draw a frequency table to show the information:
r = red, **b** = brown **x** = blonde

**r, b, b, b, b, b, x, b, x, b,
x, b, b, r, b, b, x, b, b, x,
b, b, b, r, x, r, b, b, b, b**

Handling Data

Mode

1 Look at this list of numbers and then complete the table beneath it.

4, 6, 2, 1, 3, 5, 2, 1, 1, 3, 4, 2, 1, 3, 3, 2, 4, 3, 2, 1, 4, 5, 2

1 is in the list 5 times
2 is in the list ___ times
3 is in the list ___ times
4 is in the list ___ times
5 is in the list ___ times
6 is in the list ___ times

Which number is in the mode? _____

2 What is the mode for each group?

a. 1, 0, 0, 1, 0, 1, 1, 0, 1, 0, 1 _____

b. $\frac{1}{2}, \frac{1}{4}, \frac{1}{2}, \frac{3}{4}, \frac{1}{4}, \frac{1}{2}, \frac{1}{2}, \frac{3}{4}, \frac{1}{2}$ _____

c. 0.5, 0.75, 0.25, 0.75, 0.25, 0.5, 0.75 _____

d. 25%, 50%, 50%, 50%, 25%, 75% _____

3 What is the mode for each group:

a. □, □, △, □, ○, △, □, ○, ○ _____

b. e, i, o, u, a, a, e, o, e, e, e, u, e, i _____

c. 5p, 10p, 1p, 10p, 5p, 10p, 5p, 5p, 10p, 1p, 10p _____

4 What is the mode of each group – there may be more than one.

a. 6, 1, 5, 2, 4, 6, 5, 1, 4, 2, 5, 6 _____

b. 4, 1, 2, 0, 1, 4, 5, 6, 2, 1, 0, 3, 0, 1 _____

c. $\frac{1}{2}, \frac{1}{4}, \frac{1}{4}, \frac{3}{4}, \frac{1}{2}, \frac{1}{2}, \frac{3}{4}, \frac{1}{4}$ _____

d. red, white, blue, blue, white _____

Handling Data

Median

1 Arrange these numbers in order with the smallest number first and then work out the median.

2, 5, 1, 9, 7, 8, 3

_____ _____

What is the median in each group?

  a. 5, 7, 2, 2, 4 _____

  b. 3, 1, 9, 7, 8, 1, 4, 9, 6 _____

  c. 2, 5, 9, 7, 8, 3, 7, 6, 4, 2, 9 _____

  d. 20, 10, 5, 10, 20, 50, 5, 10, 20, 10, 20 _____

2 What is the median in each group?

  a. $\frac{1}{2}, \frac{3}{4}, \frac{1}{4}$, _____

  b. 17, 42, 9, 67, 12, 92, 68 _____

  c. 40, 80, 90, 10, 70, 50, 30 _____

  d. 1, 0, 0, 1, 1, 1, 1, 0, 0, 0, 1 _____

3 The median of 2, 4, 5, 7, is half way between 4 and 5 which is $4\frac{1}{2}$. Work out the median of each of these groups.

  a. 6, 12, 7, 2 _____

  b. 4, 1, 5, 2, 4, 6, 7, 9 _____

  c. 0, 1, 0, 1, 0, 1, 0, 1 _____

  d. 10, 50, 30, 60 _____

  e. 17, 13, 19, 21 _____

  f. 100, 70, 40, 80, 20, 10 _____

Level 4

5

4

6

TOTAL

Handling Data

Diagrams/equal intervals

1. Look at this frequency diagram and then answer the questions.

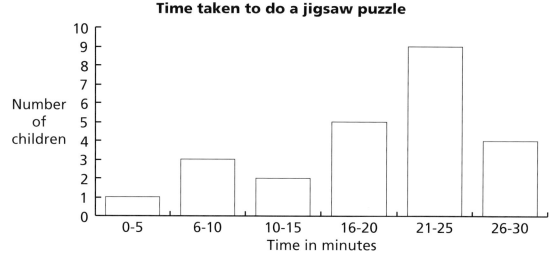

Time taken to do a jigsaw puzzle

a. How many children took 5 minutes or less? _____

b. How many children took more than 20 minutes? _____

c. How many children took between 10 and 20 minutes? _____

d. How many children did the jigsaw puzzle altogether? _____

2. Draw a frequency diagram to show this information.

50 children were given a spelling test of 50 words. These are the number of questions these children got right.

4, 15, 42, 23, 27, 48, 31, 22, 49, 31, 25, 31, 7, 32, 48, 27, 32, 45, 25, 28, 43, 19, 26, 17, 35, 26, 18, 24, 27, 30, 26, 21, 24, 34, 2, 15, 32, 41, 47, 28, 24, 34, 40, 18, 12, 32, 1, 3, 49, 26

Handling Data

Line graphs/probability

Level 4

1 This line graph shows the temperature in a fridge from the time when it is first turned on. Finish the graph using the information beneath it.

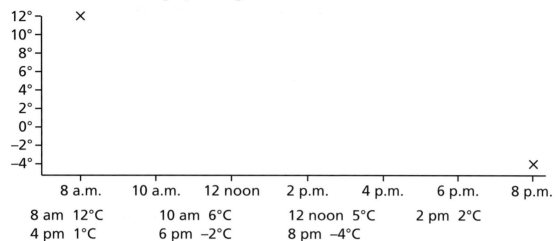

| 8 am 12°C | 10 am 6°C | 12 noon 5°C | 2 pm 2°C |
| 4 pm 1°C | 6 pm −2°C | 8 pm −4°C | |

2 Look at this line graph and then answer the questions.

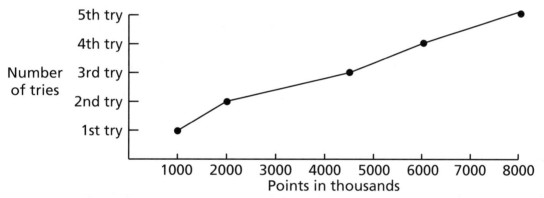

a. What was the score on the third try? _____

b. How much did the score rise between the first and the last tries?

_____

c. How much did the score rise between the 3rd and 4th tries?

_____

3 Put each of the events on to this probability line.

Impossible — Unlikely — Fair chance — Likely — Certain

a. 4 is between 3 and 5.

b. You will be chased by a crocodile.

c. You can fit into a matchbox.

d. If you throw a 1p coin it will come up heads.

TOTAL

Handling Data

Mean

1 Work out the mean of each pair of numbers.

a. 6 and 8 _____   b. 4 and 10 _____   c. 5 and 7 _____

d. 10 and 10 _____   e. 10p and 20p _____   f. 2p and 10p _____

g. 50p and 20p _____   h. 25p and 35p _____

2 Work out the mean of each group of numbers.

a. 1, 3, 5 _____   b. 2, 7, 9 _____   c. 4, 8, 18 _____

d. 10, 40, 20, 30 _____   e. £10, £5, £20, £15 _____

f. 8 m, 6 m, 10 m, 4 m, 12 m _____

3 a. The mean of three numbers is 15. Two of the numbers are 5 and 10.

What is the third number? _____

b. The mean of four numbers is 8. Three of the numbers are 2, 7 and 11.

What is the fourth number? _____

4 Three children have taken some tests. These are the results:

James 4, 7, 8, 11   Alice 6, 8, 8, 6   Ben 9, 7, 5, 11

Which child had the highest mean score? _____

5 This bar graph shows the scores of three quiz teams.

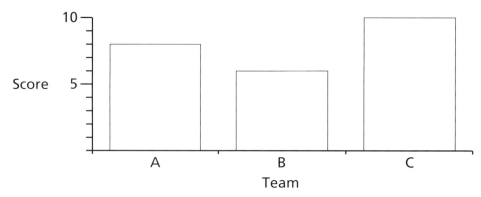

a. What was the mean score of the three teams? _____

b. Which team had the same as the mean score? _____

Handling Data

Mean/range/comparisons

Level 5

1 These are the temperatures at noon on five days in July.

        15°   18°   24°   20°   23°

  a. What is the mean temperature? _____

  b. What is the range of the temperatures? _____

  c. How many days were colder than the mean temperature? _____

3

2 Ten teachers give out these house points in a week.

    20   32   19   41   35
    26   30   17   22   18

  a. What is the mean number of house points? _____

  b. What is the range of the house points given? _____

  c. How many teachers gave more than the mean number? _____

3

3 These are the scores of two quiz teams over 5 rounds

	Round 1	Round 2	Round 3	Round 4	Round 5
Team A	7	6	7	8	7
Team B	9	8	7	8	8

  a. What was the mean score of each team? _____

  b. Which team had the highest mean score? _____

  c. What was the range of each team? _____

  d. What was the mean score of both teams combined? _____

  e. Which round had the mean score of 7.5? _____

5

TOTAL

Handling Data

Pie charts

1 Favourite flavours of ice cream

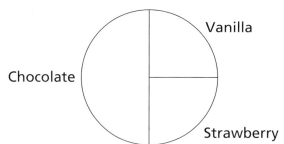

a. Which was the most popular flavour? _____

b. 28 children were asked what flavour they liked.

   How many preferred strawberry? _____

c. How many children did not prefer vanilla? _____

2 32 children were asked what their favourite colour was.

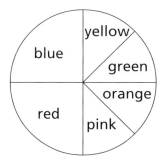

a. What fraction of the children preferred blue? _____

b. What fraction of the children preferred orange? _____

c. How many children preferred red? _____

d. How many children preferred yellow? _____

e. Which two colours were joint favourite? _____

3 These pie charts show the children who prefer either Maxi-Cola or Moca-Cola in 2 classes.

6M has 32 children
6P has 24 children

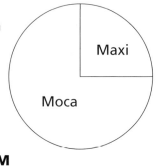

6 M

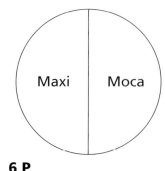

6 P

How many more children in 6P prefer Maxi-cola than in 6M? _____